DON'T LET YOUR KIDS KILL YOU

*A Guide for Parents
of Drug and Alcohol
Addicted Children*

Charles Rubin

NEW CENTURY PUBLISHERS

Sonoma County, California • London, England

This NewCentury Publishers Edition copyright © 2011
Charles Rubin

First published in USA, Great Britain, Australia, Spain, Brazil,
France, Slovakia

Original copyright © 1996 Charles Rubin

Library of Congress-in-Publishing Data

Rubin, Charles
Don't let your kids kill you: a survival guide for parents of
drug addicts and alcoholics/ Charles Rubin
3rd ed.
Includes index
LCCN: 2007930494
ISBN: 978-0-9679790-5-2

1. Parents of alcoholics. 2. Parents of narcotic addicts.
3. Alcoholics—Family relationships.
4. Narcotics addicts—Family relationships. 1.Title

HV5132R83   606.86′19
QB103-536

Cover Design: Izumi Motai

Printed in the United States of America
3rd Edition
14 15 16 17 18 19 20

NewCentury Publishers
P.O. Box 750265
Petaluma, CA 94975
Tel: 707 769 9808
Email: NewCentPub.com
www.NewCenturyPublishers.com

For my dear wife, Betty

Acknowledgment

In memory of my beloved wife, Betty Bethards, author ("The Dream Book: Symbols of Self Understanding" and other books) and spiritual leader, who inspired me to write this book, and to all the parents, parents' groups, treatment centers, rehabilitation centers, therapists, 12-step groups, and teachers who have found value in these pages. Additionally, to those who know of the tragedy and waste created by drug and alcohol abuse, and have had the courage to face the problems instead of sweeping them under the carpet.

CONTENTS

FOREWORD

At the time that I wrote *Don't Let Your Kids Kill You: A Guide for Parents of Drug and Alcohol Addicted Children*, I was living in a state of desperation due to two kids on drugs. In order to get through the day to day onslaught, I wrote for myself a personal guide that would not only allow me to deal with the unrelieved emotional stress, but one that might help me strive for some measure of happiness and fulfillment in this bleakest of circumstances.

I hadn't intended this guide for publication but when I mentioned it to my agent, the legendary Ben Kamsler, he predicted that it would be in every home in America. I now think that what he meant was that this book *belonged* in every home in America. He knew that children all over the country (and the world for that matter) were succumbing to the drug pandemic which was wrecking the lives of countless millions of people, both the children and their families.

There are many helpful books and programs available that focus solely on the erring child, but *Don't Let Your Kids Kill You* is the only book available for parents and parents alone. It's a source that gives parents the help and motivation they need to nurture and believe in themselves and to treasure their own lives. Some critics might have seen this as a selfish quest, but not only do the parents benefit through a program of taking care of themselves, but their children benefit as well. It is only through parents becoming conscious of their own needs and living as positive a life as possible that anything can change.

The position that dares suggest parents have a right to a good life is, at times, contrary to what a great portion of our society believes. The accepted behavior, in social terms, is for parents with kids on drugs to go around like zombies, neglecting their work and the rest of their families and of course, themselves, so as to steep themselves in misery over what their drug-induced kids might be up to.

Making that position worse is a government that spends millions on TV spots that point the finger at the parent as someone who hasn't raised his or her child right and who has to take ultimate responsibility and blame for this lack of guidance. These spots drone on about how parents are supposed to talk to their children about drugs. A parent can talk to a child who is on drugs until he or she is blue in the face. This is like trying to talk to a child about sex. In both cases, it's pretty clear from today's information revolution that even an fifth-grader can provide us with far more details than we can provide him or her.

So when my agent persuaded me to publish my personal guide—which was saving me from hell—I was only too happy to comply. In the first printing, there were two reactions: One from parents who were incredibly relieved to find such a book, and another from the parents who were frightened to death by the title and premise. With the latter group, just going to the cashier with such a book struck fear into their hearts—what would the cashier think? For that matter what would relatives and neighbors and coworkers think? Would the parent just laugh nervously if discovered reading this book and would he or she blush a scarlet hue and say the book was for someone else? Would the secret that the parent harbored a child doing drugs be revealed to the world?

There were parents who read the book on the sly. I even thought of marketing it in a plain brown wrapper. But with the rapid increase in children succumbing to substances and the present situation when drug-taking is at an all-time high (no pun intended), many of these parents are now overlooking any prior reservations about safeguarding "the secret and shame of having drug-ridden children", and the book has become even more in demand.

Of course, there are still some parents who shirk

any possibility of being discovered. I get calls and emails regularly from parents who absolutely refuse to identify themselves, but at the same time, desperately want advice on how to stay sane, stay alive.

Don't Let Your Kids Kill You is not only a book, but a companion you can refer to on a daily basis. I know, from what many parents have told me, that the reason this book is a successful resource is that it is written by someone just like them. Someone who had suffered great pain and confusion due to the choices made by a beloved child.

And so, here it is, the newly revised *Don't Let Your Kids Kill You: A Guide for Parents of Drug and Alcohol Addicted Children* with further insights and information.

Charles Rubin
Sonoma County, California

INTRODUCTION

Don't Let Your kids Kill You is a book for parents, written by a parent. But it's not for just any parent. The fact is, unless you happen to be one of the rapidly growing numbers of mothers and fathers whose lives have been seriously disrupted by a drug or alcohol-addicted[1] child—young, adolescent, or adult—there is little chance you'll be able to relate to what is written in these pages. That's because parents of addicted children experience situations that differ nearly beyond belief from those experienced by parents of non-addicted children.

As the first and only book on the market that focuses solely on the hurting parent and not the erring child, *Don't Let Your Kids Kill You* takes the radical view that parents are not, regardless of popular thought, the architects of the raging addicts their kids have become. It defies generalized judgments that parents are to blame for the choices made by their children. (I am not, of course, including in this statement the parents with a history of legally accountable sexual, physical, or emotional abuse toward their children. I am in no way qualified to advise those parents, nor can I estimate how much they may have damaged their young.)

What this book emphasizes is that it isn't our children who are bad, but the drugs they use. This is an important fact to remember, especially when facing the insidious nature of drugs and the results of drug use in a child. Imagine opening a closet door and finding, on the floor, a child curled up in a fetal position with his bong. Or returning home after work to discover holes in the wall large enough to slide a dishwasher through—with no one being able to explain how they got there. Or finding one's bank account tampered with and hundreds or even thousands of dollars missing. Or the terror that reigns in a household when the addicted child is able to physically brutalize parents and other family members.

Like many parents who've dealt with drug or alcohol-addicted children, I found myself living a nightmarish existence as my children descended deeper and deeper into unreachable areas. In most cases, kids on drugs metamorphose into abusive, violent, foulmouthed, anti-social individuals. Such kids do not respects rules, laws, or personal property. They're not only self-destructive, but seemingly intent on destroying everything around them, including the people who care most about them. It is little wonder that the stress upon parents can lead to divorce, career upsets, strokes, heart attacks, and early death.

Grainger Brown, a family counselor in Helena, Montana, who has worked with chemically-addicted children and their parents much of his career, describes the trauma of a parent trying to save his or her addicted child as equal to the trauma of a combat veteran who has blamed himself for the war.

As if this monumental self-blame and self-condemnation aren't enough, the mainstream of society is just as eager to point the finger, placing all responsibility for the child's actions squarely on the parent's shoulders, compounding the problem even further. An example of this type parent-hounding occurred not long ago when the courts in a small community in Oregon ruled that should a child commit a felony, it would be the parents who'd be charged. The message to addicted kids couldn't have been clearer: Go out and raise hell—we'll just go after your parents. In other words, if the kids do the crime, the parents do the time.

And who said parents can't follow their kids around every moment of the day? In Ohio, a mother was ordered *chained* to her drug-addicted daughter in an effort to curtail the youngster's negative activities. It is not surprising that the mother had a stroke shortly after this court order and died. At which point the judge ordered the father to take her place.

For Los Angeles clinical hypnotherapist and Ph.D, Shira Deitsch, whose clients include many parents of addicts, the critical question, the one *Don't Let Your Kids Kill You* raises is: What actions are parents supposed to take when loyalty to their children becomes their downfall?

Don't Let Your Kids Kill You answers this question and shows parents how they can salvage their lives. Through relating my own experiences with drug-dependent children as well as those of other parents, this book lets parents know that they are not alone in their confusion and grief. At the very least, the pages of this book will help dissolve their sense of isolation along with the conviction that the addictions of their young are the results of poor parenting.

Others that *Don't Let Your Kids Kill You* is designed to serve are therapists, psychologists, educators, and social workers. This book can also help prepare far-thinking parents of non-addicts who realize that, in today's world of increasing drug and alcohol use, it could happen to their children, too.

The audience for this book is wider still—and larger than I ever imagined. I refer to the spouses, children, siblings, and friends of people on drugs and alcohol, many of whom don't even have children. The tenets of *Don't Let Your Kids Kill You* would apply just as much were the title to change to *Don't Let Your Kids, Parents, Siblings, Friends, Lovers, Boss, or Anyone Else, for that Matter, Kill You.*

Also...

At a time when drug use in our young is at epidemic proportions, it is essential that people understand that this is not just a crisis facing parents, but a crisis that is facing all of us worldwide.

Drug use is much less a parental problem than it is a governmental and societal problem. Society uses drugs, and it is up to government to protect society against itself. If this was a case of our reservoirs being poisoned, we'd act swiftly to end the problem. Yet we go on allowing our children to be poisoned by any number of drugs coming into our country on a daily basis, along with home-made substances.

If parents and government could work together, a difference could be made. Ideas on what you can do to make that difference can be found in the last chapter of this book...

Note

1. The term "drugs" applies to any chemical, including alcohol, that alters a person's mental, physical, and emotional state, as stated in *The International Classification of Diseases*, 4th edition, the 9th revision, published by McGraw Hill for the World Health Organization.

1

Take a Good Look at Yourself

MY STORY. There was a time in my life when I felt like the luckiest man on earth. I was the father of two wonderful sons who gave me endless joy. These boys, so different from one another, were to me one-of-a-kind treasures. I valued and marveled at their differences. One was gregarious and bright with a foghorn voice so unusual in a young child. The other was quietly powerful, someone to whom you gave instant respect, a born leader. But, as time went on, it became apparent that they had one very distinct feature in common: a propensity for chemical addiction.

Those small children are now gone without a trace. One minute they were right there in my life and the next minute they'd grown into adolescents.

And what I originally had mistaken as the typically bizarre behavior of two puberty-age boys (the signs of which Dr. Spock cautions parents to be on the lookout for) was actually the unbelievably gruesome side-effects of substance abuse.

Like many parents who eventually discover the real reasons behind the blatant, off-the-wall behavior of their kids, I didn't know how to handle the situation. It had never occurred to me that my kids might become drug addicts. Naivete or lack of awareness or just plain ignorance had been my cushion and suddenly there was nothing between me and the truth.

What finally got through to me regarding my relationship with my kids was that I hadn't seen or heard from their true selves in a very long time. Those two delightful small children had transformed into other beings. Over a period of several years, they'd become their drugs, nothing more. Increasingly, it became impossible to communicate with them as I knew them because those two people had disappeared. They'd vacated their bodies the way someone might vacate an old house. Also abandoned was all that was warm, unique, friendly, and familiar about them.

Taking up residence now were the addicts: predatory and ill-natured personifications of drugs and alcohol. If I'd come into contact with strangers demonstrating these characteristics, I would have run a million miles to escape the aura of negativity emanating from them.

To run from strangers is one thing. To run from one's own children is another. Yet, that is precisely what I knew I had to do in order to survive. Because not only had I got a realistic picture of what my children had become, I had a realistic picture of what I had become. And the picture was frightening.

Due to stress and worry, I was physically troubled with mysterious ailments such as numbness in both arms and alarming fatigue. I'd lost weight and had a grayish pallor. Mentally, I had trouble remembering what I was supposed to be doing at any given moment, and I couldn't concentrate on my work. My marriage, which had not been strong for some time, faltered completely under the pressures brought upon us—not by the addictions of our sons, but by the inability to deal with those addictions as a unified couple.

I stayed in this picture for quite a few years, feeling the impact of each negative action by my kids as an almost physical assault upon me. Eventually, seeing how destructive this situation was, I had no choice but to let go of my children (who were, by this time, no longer children). They were now young adults and I'd been doing this terrible dance with them for the previous half dozen years. I'd stuck around long enough.

Letting go meant, in effect, that I would be

letting them make their mistakes and that I would neither try to dissuade them nor rescue them. All the time, energy, and other outlay I'd put into them would now be curtailed and redirected toward myself. No one says it's easy to restructure one's life, especially when the focus has always been on the addicted child. But there has to be a shift if anything is going to be salvaged. The *focal point* has to fall upon the *parent* instead of the addict.

My sons are now in their late twenties. One of them has made incredible strides to beat his addictions and has been "clean and sober" for at least five years, for which I am grateful. My other son lives far away, but I usually know when he's addiction-free: He'll pop on the phone with that same foghorn voice, sounding joyous and loving as he did all those years ago. Unfortunately, those times are rare.

I care about my sons every bit as much as I did when they were small, but today, I also care about a third person whom I'd neglected for a long time. Myself.

What price parenthood?

If you're like a lot of parents who've been living out a horror film, with your drugged or drunken kids assuming the starring roles, you're probably a wreck mentally, physically, and spiritually, not to mention financially. And because parenthood is so often identified with suffering and sacrifice, perhaps you don't even recognize the state you're in. Or perhaps you do recognize it and simply accept it as the price one pays to be a parent. Such acceptance can be defeatist as well as unnecessary. Worst of all, it can be suicidal.

When you're at the mercy of an abusive person, in ways over which you have no control, or in ways that you allow through passivity, you can find yourself nervous, cranky, and apprehensive. You may be prone to physical and emotional ills as well as financial ruin, and possibly even die from the overwhelming stress of it all.

And when that abusive person turns out to be your own child, the toll upon you can double. Wondering what catastrophe your child is going to create next is enough to have you jumping out of your skin every time the phone rings. How many times has it been the police informing you that your son or daughter has been arrested again? Or an outraged neighbor complaining of some misdemeanor perpetrated by your child? Or your child's school informing you that you'll have to come in right away to discuss the latest in a series of anti-social acts carried out by your child? Or one of your child's friends who uses your home like a gas station toilet? Or that voice on the phone you've come to recognize as your child's drug connection?

Believe it or not, the stress you feel from these encounters can kill you.

How much can a body take?

According to Dr. Mark Fahey, M.D., of Santa Rosa, California, stress transforms the body's focus from normal homeostasis, the relaxed state, to one of total tension, a fight-or-flight response. All food stores in the body are sacrificed to provide quick energy. Your heart rate and blood pressure go up trying to deliver this food to the muscles. Constant stress can lead to weight loss, fatigue, increased incidence of heart "burnout" which in turn can lead to chest pain, heart attacks, and arrhythmias leading to sudden death.

Medical science is finding more and more that stress plays a part in causing other diseases such as cancer. For when a person suppresses emotions, as parents of addicts often do, the body becomes more vulnerable.

In effect, stress involves the entire body. And there is no stress worse than that of a parent agonizing over the child who has become incapacitated through drug addiction or alcoholism.

What exactly is an addict?

If you can understand the effect chemicals have on a person, you'll have an idea of what you're up against when your son or daughter becomes an addict. First of all, substance abuse is not, as many parents believe, merely the manifestation of a willful personality. It is an uncontrollable craving, as much a mental and emotional need as a physical one. When your addict is underage, you have a better chance of getting him or her help, although addicts of all ages usually find ways to return to substances no matter what help you give them.

Addicts are not criminals, but the substances in their bodies often make them into criminals. Mind-altering drugs can transform the mildest personality into the most violent. In today's world, drugs and guns seem to go hand in hand, making life dangerous for everyone. In effect, drugs and alcohol remove all priorities in a person's life such as school, friends, relationships, and plans for the future. The person you know is replaced with someone whose behavior is totally unlike that of your loved one. This is a stranger who, because of the drugs, will lie to you and steal from you repeatedly, make promises that will never be kept, and abuse you verbally, emotionally, and physically at the slightest provocation. You cannot trust an addict. He or she may look just like the child you used to trust, but otherwise, there are no similarities as long as substances are being used.

An addict is someone who stamps all the niceties of life into the ground with a ferocity that's unbounded. Somewhere within that addict there may be the knowledge that what he or she is doing is destructive, but because of the strong attraction to euphoria and escape, the addict is either unwilling or unable to seek a change. I think that some of the bravest people in the world are those addicts who manage to grasp a hold on sobriety and stay with it, even though the temptation to return to substances is a daily occurrence.

Unless an addict has a true desire to kick the habit, there is nothing you can do to bring back the person within. What is heartbreaking for the parent is the inability to accept the self-destructiveness of the addict, a very real and tragic circumstance. Instead of dealing with addictions as a disease,[1] many parents adapt to the Dr. Jekyll / Mr. Hyde manifestations of it. And live that way, if you can call existing in a constant state of fear and apprehension living.

Bargaining with the addict:
You may as well save your breath

Trying to negotiate with an addict never works. The effect of substances on the human brain render it useless in terms of keeping agreements. Often, the addict won't even *remember* he or she made a pact of any kind with you. Or, if there is no memory lapse, the addict might simply "blow off" his or her part of the agreement. And then tell you where to go if you protest.

I know of one father who actually gave his addicted son money to stay off drugs. What was this father thinking? The son just used the money to buy more drugs.

If you think you can work out a deal with your addicted child, you may as well try it. The problem is that some parents keep "trying it." They allow their addicted kids the run of the home. Or they buy their addicted kids cars. Or they pay off their addicted kids' debts. This is in return for the promise that the addict will change his or her ways and live like a normal member of society. The addict will happily make such a promise—why turn down a generous offer?—but almost never keep it. Parents soon realize that "bribing" the addict generates nothing but further frustration and disappointment.

Still think you can have a normal relationship with an addict?

Sorry. It's impossible. If you could understand the dynamics of your link with an addicted child and the destructive power it has over you, you might be able to embark upon a workable solution. The first thing you must realize is that the relationship between you and the addict, as strong as it may seem, has in actuality been terminated by whatever substance is in your child's body.

This doesn't mean you can't have a hostage/child relationship if you really want one. That's a booby prize, but many parents go for it.

However, if this is your situation and you're

tiring of it, you can take steps to release yourself as
the hostage you so willingly allowed yourself to become. Even in relatively trouble-free parent/child
relationships, there's always a certain amount of
emotional pressure (for the parent to concede to the
child's wishes) due to the strong nature of the bond.
But in the case of the parent/addict relationship, the
parent is usually under the control of the addict.
Which is just the way the addict likes it.

From my own experience, I would say that enjoying a normal relationship with an addicted child
with chemicals coursing through his or her veins
isn't going to happen. This is true for several reasons. The first is that the parent may still be acting
out a fantasy that perhaps, someday, the addict
will execute a complete turnaround and start doing things the way the parent prefers. The second
reason has to do with the addict who, because of his
or her need to use, actively depends on the parent as
a source of revenue.

The parent (who has no one else to try to mold)
and the child (who has no one else to lash out
at, blame, and abuse) can remain in this painfully
suffocating mode. This pattern continues until the
parent grasps how destructive the relationship has
been (which might be never) or until the child miraculously becomes a healthy, motivated member of
society (which also might be never).

Still think you can have a relationship with an addict? Read on.

A drug called denial

Okay, here's the scenario. You have a child (for simplicity's sake, I'll use the masculine form) of roughly twenty-one years old. You always thought that by this milestone in his life he'd be finishing a degree and starting a career. But he has no job and is a high school dropout. He spends his days (and nights) with friends who like to drink and/or take drugs and listen to ear-shattering heavy metal or rap (in your living room) until all hours of the night and early morning. He complains about how society has mistreated him, rips off government service agencies whenever possible, and abuses just about everybody in sight—especially you.

How close did I come to describing the addict in your home?

Many parents live in a state of denial when it comes to themselves and their kids. Denial can be like some kind of impenetrable fortress that allows nothing to get through. Even when parents are continually presented with evidence in all shapes and forms that their kids are deeply entrenched in negative pastimes, they refuse to look. These parents are too believing, too green to possibly conceive of their children—the children from whom they'd had such high expectations—doing anything so grossly wrong.

Denial, as I have realized, is a strong force that at first protects many parents from the painful recognition that their children have somehow become less-than-sterling characters engaged in less-than-sterling endeavors. The inability to see the situation clearly allowed me to live in a state of prolonged delusion, a kind of slow roasting over an open fire. But when the denial finally evaporated, I was left with nothing but raw, all-consuming heartache. Finally waking up, I saw that my kids were virtual veterans in the shady world of drug and alcohol addiction.

As I was to find out at a much later date, my children had been predisposed toward substances through a long history of alcoholism on both sides of the family. But at the time that I was first exposed to the workings of these substances upon my children, I had no idea how serious the problem was. Like many parents before and after me, I was too ignorant of the treacherous effects of drug and alcohol addiction to know how to handle it.

A word about manipulation: yours

Dealing with an addict forces you to abandon all the old strategies that worked so well when your child was younger.

Like most parents, you were something of a manipulator yourself. However, when the addict became your equal, you were rendered powerless.

Suddenly, nothing worked. You found you weren't in control any longer. You couldn't get the addict to give up drugs or go into a rehab or get a job or even a haircut. He just laughed in your face. This gave you, for the first time in your life, a view of how underhanded you might have been trying to get the addict to do what you wanted.

You tried the silent treatment, the hurt treatment, the aloof treatment. And you found the addict was still jabbing needles into his veins. Maybe just to tune you out.

It's been quite a rude awakening, being outsmarted on every level by someone whose diapers you used to change.

Reacting against the addict: It doesn't work

Instead of "handling" the problems that arose—and there were many—I reacted against them. These reactions took the form of exasperated outbursts followed by grievous internalizing. I reacted against the truancy reports that started to flood in. I reacted against the violent outbursts and tirades my drug-crazed kids leveled against their mom and me on a regular basis. I reacted against the sudden absences and loss of family possessions, undoubtedly hocked in order to pay for drugs. I reacted against the missing money, the forged checks, the stolen credit cards, the wrecked cars, the ruined public property. I reacted against the utter destruction that was wreaked upon our house: the broken windows, damaged furniture, doors off the hinges, badly trampled grounds, the free-standing garage that was knocked of its foundation by someone trying to maneuver (while under the influence of some substance or other) a vehicle through its doors. But most of all, I reacted against the all-powerful force of drugs and alcohol that was in the process of destroying the love we'd all felt for one another. As someone who was totally oriented toward family values and togetherness, I was witness to the heartbreaking spectacle of my beloved family being ripped apart.

But throughout all this, my denial was such that I still had faith that a miracle would take place, restoring our family to the way we'd once been: happy, close-knit, building for the future. These dreams and hopes were never realized.

Workaholism: another kind of obsession

When parents are obsessed with their kids, they're not able to concentrate on much else.

Or, just the opposite can happen. A parent can adopt another obsession called work. It's easy to do this because at work there are always assignments to complete, deadlines to be met, challenges to be won.

Of course, the dangers inherent in using one's job as an escape from family problems is that soon the job problems become all-consuming in themselves and efficiency goes out the window. The workaholic has effectively switched one obsession for another. When such fanaticism becomes too much for everyone at the place of business, the workaholic parent may find him or herself looking for another job.

Hey, where did all your friends go?

There comes a time when obsessed parents find that their friends are avoiding them. These friends simply don't want to hear one more grisly episode on what the addicted kids are doing. It's too depressing. Any compassion they may have offered at first has long since waned. Their eyes say what their mouths don't always: that the problems of addicted kids aren't easy to listen to day after day, month after month, year after year.

Friends like to discuss something other than tragedy. They like to discuss the latest movie or sports or where to go on vacation. If there's no room in a parent's life for the lighter things and if all the friends are going to hear is more and more gloom and doom, they will probably want to take a break from the friendship, perhaps even permanently. They're the gauge parents of addicts need in order to see how isolated they've become in their obsessed state.

If you've come to this juncture in your life, it's time to look at these obsessions. Because not only do they wreck careers and friendships. They also wreck marriages.

Hey, where did your marriage go?

The pressures that parents allow addicted children to place upon them are very likely to cause deterioration in a very vulnerable area—the marriage. As so often happens when children are in trouble, the parents have a serious falling out with one another. A lot of blame and accusation goes on. Many parents fall into a routine of daily combat which eventually leads to a parting of the ways.

It doesn't matter, in these cases, who's right and who's wrong. Mothers tend to see their children as being too young and innocent to understand the seriousness of their actions. They're far more willing to give the child new opportunities to mend his or her ways. In a dysfunctional relationship between mother and child, the mother will often take the blame for what's happening or blame the child's father. Very little, if anything, is resolved.

Fathers, so it seems, are less willing to mollify their errant kids. This is probably because the male in society is expected to be less emotional, more pragmatic than the female. If the father has developed too far in this direction, he can become militaristic—which is anathema to the nurturing mother. She may question his way of letting their kids suffer the consequences of their choices. And he may become angered for what appears to be excessive babying of the addict on the mother's part.

What's needed for a stable partnership between mothers and fathers is an equal balance of feminine/ masculine energy. The big problem arises when either partner is expected by the other to adapt to his or her way when dealing with the addicted child. If the parents are so totally opposed to one another's views, it will be almost impossible to bring about the solutions necessary to benefit the relationship and keep it functioning.

In a family where there's dissension, it's often the addicted child who is keeping both parents sparring. This manipulative maneuver by the child takes, to some extent, the onus off him or herself. While the parents are busy battling each other, the addicted child has more opportunity to continue his or her unhealthy pastimes. Though many parents would find it hard to accept such a concept, the fact is that an addicted child will seize every chance possible to benefit from the parents' confusion and strife. The further parents withdraw from one another, the more power the addicted child has. In this position, the addict can do exactly what he or she wants with the family and within the family.

It's important in any marriage where there is an addicted child that the parents avoid clashing in their individual philosophies. They can only do this by *joining together in a stronger show of force*, a secure and united front, one which the addicted child cannot undermine or penetrate. It's a shame when the parents aren't able to work things out between them, either on their own or with the help and wisdom of a therapist. And it's very sad if they allow their love for one another to become clouded with bitterness and anger.

Taking control of the situation

There are a great many parents—as I've learned by attending endless parent support group meetings—who had the same high hopes for their families as I. If you're such a parent, then you probably know that it isn't just the child who can be out of control, but also the parent. Possibly you are also aware that continuous reacting on your part is useless as well as extremely hazardous to your health and well-being.

The most ruinous thing you can do is to allow the situation to continue on its present destructive course. Here are some simple steps you can take to deactivate the negativity so rampant in your family dynamics. Please note that it takes courage and determination to carry this off successfully.

1. Cut off all funds to the addict. Holding onto the purse strings with an iron fist will have immediate results, as well as repercussions. (Keep an eye on family valuables. In fact, lock them away.)

2. Cut off all privileges accorded to your addicts—such as use of the family car or having their friends in your house.

3. Carry out all threats you make. The fastest way to lose credibility with addicted children is to become a "softie" at the last minute.

4. Refuse to rescue your addicts when they get into legal jams. Don't pay their fines or their bail.

5. Get yourself into a support group such as Al-Anon, Nar-Anon, Parents Anonymous, or Tough Love as fast as you can.

6. Attempt to get your addicted kids into rehabs. If they're underage you can sign them in. Adult admission is done on a voluntary basis, so you may be out of luck.

7. Drugs erase any trace of conscience. Be aware that many of today's drugged youths will think nothing of injuring or even murdering their parents for money. If you suspect that your child could resort to this level of violence, get in touch with the police.

If you're a single parent there will be one voice, but if you're married there'll be two. It's important to merge those two voices so that a single, clear message reaches the addict. If you can work with your partner as a team to institute these simple steps when dealing with the addict, you'll have done yourself and your family a great service.

If, however, you entertain the notion that you were responsible for your child's addictions in the first place, chances are you won't be effective in enforcing these guidelines. That's what the next chapter is all about.

Note

1. Drug abuse and alcoholism are officially listed in *The International Classification of Diseases*, 4th edition, 9th revision, the World Health Organization's directory on diseases.

2

Do You Really Think You Did This to Your Kids?

NANCY'S STORY. The first thing I notice about this single-parent mother of two is her body language. Nancy sits across from me in a rigid, semi-defensive pose. When she speaks, she seems to have trouble meeting my gaze. It's as though she's harboring some awful secret. But it isn't a secret at all, as she will relate in her story. The discomfort she's expressing has to do with her heavily addicted daughter. And the terrible thing she's harboring is guilt.

I know something about her from information supplied by mutual friends. The main dynamic in her life seems to be the blame she places upon herself for the way things have turned out for her daughter, Hilary. When Hilary was six years old and her brother Ben was four, Nancy took them from Miami to Atlanta—leaving behind forever an alcoholic and abusive husband and father.

In Atlanta, as the forty-two-year-old Nancy now

explains, she worked two jobs to put herself through nursing school and to pay for day care.

"It was a tough eight years," Nancy says. "I was always working or going to school and I didn't see the kids much. But as least I was able to buy this house and give Hilary and Ben a decent neighborhood to grow up in. If I'd stayed with my husband in Miami, there's no telling where any of us would be today. Or in what condition. Burt had been jobless, alcoholic, and violent. He had a terrible temper and would often use physical force on me and the kids. I got us out of there when I suspected he might sexually assault Hilary."

Even with all she's done for her family, Nancy feels responsible for the fact that Hilary, now seventeen, is a seasoned heroin abuser who pays for her habit through dealing drugs herself. Nancy bases her ever-present feeling of guilt and remorse on several factors. The first is that she didn't spend enough time at home with Hilary during the girl's formative years. The second is a history of drug addiction in Nancy's family, which she fears may have been passed on to Hilary.

"And then there's Hilary's father who is an alcoholic," says Nancy.

As for her other child, Ben, Nancy is incredibly grateful for the way he's turned out. According to her, he's well-adjusted, cheerful, and a top student at his high school.

"He's very supportive of me," Nancy says. "I don't know what I would have done without him. I mean, I didn't spend a lot of time with him, either, as he was growing up, but somehow he managed to stay away from drugs. I don't think it's because of me that he's so positive. Why do I feel responsible for Hilary being such a mess?"

There are thousands of kids like Hilary hooked on drugs. And there are thousands parents like Nancy who are hooked on guilt. I used to be one of them.

Egotism and parenthood

Parents must be the arch-egotists of all time. It's not enough that their children have the same blood as them, they must also have the same exact values. It's as though parents view their children as empty vessels into which they must pour a complete data base that will serve the child through life.

What many parents fail to realize is that children come out of the womb with a complete data base that's exclusively their own and which is fully operational by the time the child is in his or her teens. It is this, not the parent, which drives the child. It's true that parents have more influence on their children than any other people on earth—and may even be able to keep a kid off drugs. But that's only if the influence is in keeping with the child's own pre-programmed agenda, and only if that influence is strong enough to withstand the temptations presented to the child by other sources such as peers, TV, and society.

If parents could step off their lofty perches for a moment, they might come to recognize that *each person fulfills his or her own destiny*—whether it be good or bad—in his or her own time and unique way. As in anything else, when it comes to substance abuse, children are going to do what they're going to do. If they don't do it today, they'll do it tomorrow. Whatever the situation, it's the child who says yes or no to drugs—it's a choice. And that choice is, ultimately, answerable by the child and by no one else. So are the consequences.

Many parents and child experts will disagree with this presentation of the choice/consequence premise. However, they'll happily accept the idea of positive choices and consequences when, for example, an industrious student excels scholastically and reaps all kinds of rewards. For some reason, the parents of such a child will allow that the child's willingness to concentrate on schoolwork—a choice —has led to something excellent—a consequence. But if this same child makes another kind of choice and starts injecting heroin into his or her veins, it's not uncommon for parents to deny the child the full brunt of the "consequences." They'd rather place some or even all the blame on themselves and on the way they brought up this child.

Admitting there's a problem

The fact is, it's very painful for parents to admit to themselves, or anyone else for that matter, that their kids might have a problem with drugs. For them, it's easier to claim ownership of their children's problems and to actually talk themselves into believing that the fault is all theirs.

Here are some random thoughts that might occur to parents who can't quite connect the idea of their kids making negative choices with their having to answer for them.

1. Are you kidding? How can a mere child make such a choice? A child has neither the experience nor the maturity to make choices. A child doesn't know what he or she is doing. That's what being a child is all about!

2. Making choices isn't for children; it's for adults. Why give children the burden of having to make choices?

3. What a trauma this experience has to be for him! It could ruin his whole life. We, his parents, ought to be the ones going to jail, not him.

I spent too many years thinking thoughts just like these. My attitude was rigid. It held parents responsible for all negative acts perpetrated by their children. I reasoned that my children could not be held accountable because they were products of their upbringing. If that upbringing wasn't perfect, then I as the parent was culpable.

Conversely, the only time I was willing to relinquish the unrealistic (and as I was to find out later, dangerous) view that all their negative qualities were due to me and all their positive qualities were due to them, was when my kids did something to my liking—such as getting good grades or coming in first in a running marathon or helping an elderly person with yard work. On those occasions, I was prone to give them *all* the credit. After all, they were the brilliant ones who applied themselves and had achieved excellent results. I was merely the proud parent.

So what made me think that the same brilliant brains that were capable of accomplishing good, honorable deeds weren't capable of creating horrendous, heartbreaking ones? It takes the same amount of energy and sometimes genius to carry off either type endeavor. In some cases, it takes far more brainpower to plan and execute a negative action than it takes to plan and execute a positive one. It was probably this kind of thinking, or lack of thinking, that kept me from admitting that some rather serious mistakes were being made by my children.

Luck of the draw

Somewhere along the line, a child makes a choice to live a healthy, constructive, and worthwhile existence or one that may be just the opposite. Most parents don't know which way the kid will choose until after the fact. In the meantime, it's easier to take for granted that one's child will do the right thing than it is to consider the possible alternatives. And it's easier to praise the child for doing a good job than it is for parents, should a problem arise, to dredge up all the various emotionally charged feelings that are part and parcel of facing an offspring's addictive nature.

When a child does something that contradicts his parents' highest hopes for him, the parents may choose to edit the facts so that the impact of the child's actions is now seen in a very diffused light. This is denial at work again. Denial is one way to get through an ordeal.

Transference of guilt is another. By this method, parents can assume the burden of responsibility and guilt that rightfully belongs to the child. If they can blame themselves for the position in which the child has placed himself, they don't have to feel quite as dreadful. And, most important, the child can still appear to them as a helpless lamb with a still-untarnished potential for good.

When my children got into drugs and alcohol in their early teens, I tailor-made my own survival kit with first a vast amount of denial and then by transferring whatever I couldn't deny onto my own broader (I thought) shoulders. I viewed their addictions and their subsequent bizarre behavior as distinctly my fault. I felt that perhaps I hadn't raised them as well as I could have, which in turn may have caused them to choose a drugged existence. What other explanation could there have been? My feeling, in general, was that I had "done this to them."

Sharing blame with the addict

Taking on this guilt was my invitation for my kids to shove most of the blame my way. Any feelings that I'd been less than a great father were intercepted by them and used against me whenever possible. Presenting myself as a scapegoat allowed my children a convenient target for their rage. This dynamic, of course, delayed an early recovery for them. The longer they could blame me, the longer they could look upon themselves as innocent victims.

To actually set this up, parents have to be on some sort of power/ego trip.

In their minds, they still believe they have the utmost authority over their children. Authority carries a lot of weight when the child is young, but as the child gets older (and wiser) the influence of the parental grip lessens. The parent is usually the last to know this, however.

As a parent, I bestowed upon myself an unusual amount of power. I gave myself the job of not just being the father of these children, but also, their God. In their early lives, my children reciprocated by treating me like a God. They would be anxious for me to get home from work at night so they could regale me with stories of their day. It seemed like I was the most important person in their lives—which, sharing the honor with their mother—was true. Nobody else treated us this way. I not only liked it and got used to it, but I thought it was going to last forever. Needless to say, it didn't.

So how come some kids turn out addicted?

A parent can give his or her child all the advantages possible, all the love and nurturing, and all the guidance any child might require, and the child can still turn out to be anti-social, ungrateful, lacking in morals, and uncaring. In the same way, a bad parent can be abusive and non-supportive and yet produce the president of the United States. Some of the most eminent people have come from horrendous backgrounds while some of the most negative and infamous people on earth have been products of loving, supportive parents who strove to do the best by their children. Which goes to show how far parental influence reaches.

When I first realized that my responsibility as a parent did have a limit, I felt truly confused. And then liberated. From that time on I've been able to see that my former actions only served to keep my children and me locked in a situation in which none of us could breathe.

As influential as parents can be during the early

years of their children's lives, there comes a time when the influence switches to the peer group. This is when the child is going to stray into territories totally foreign to the parents. How easy it seems on television sitcoms for families to remain close through the most devastating situations or to show love and affection for one another when there is great conflict between them. In real life, we don't have outside scriptwriters to remedy our every family ill. We are our own scriptwriters; we have to take responsibility for all our words and actions. But we cannot take responsibility for the words and actions of others, even our children.

Always in the back of a parent's mind are these questions: Did I do this to my kids? If I had been a better parent—more caring, gentler, stronger, intuitive, healthy, compassionate, and centered— would my kids have been less prone to take drugs, drink alcohol, become violent, get into trouble with the law and in school? Would they have been more motivated, industrious, happier, and healthier individuals?

There are no guarantees. Most parents are clueless as to how their children will turn out . . . until they turn out. There are many children who, because of the enormous pain they're in over their own failings, find relief in blaming their parents for the state of things. They complain ceaselessly about how their parents did this to them and that to them.

How they made them into neurotics, bulimics, malcontents, drunks, junkies.

And just as there are many children making these accusations, there are the corresponding parents going along with it all, accepting without question the judgments and condemnations. The act of accusing one's parents for every misfortune that has occurred has become popular sport. With the parent the willing prey.

No parent is *completely* blameless

Obviously, each parent must search his or her heart to see if there is evidence to substantiate the child's accusations. At one time or another, all parents are abusive toward their children. Paddling a child's bottom can be construed as abusive. Raising one's voice to a child can be construed as abusive. Belittling a child or undermining that child's self-confidence in any way can be construed as abusive.

Soul searching provides the confused parent with some pertinent truths. And one of those truths may be that yes, you weren't exactly the model parent. Perhaps you were impatient with your kids or insensitive to their needs. Perhaps you didn't spend enough time with them or give them the affection they needed. There are many issues with which to beat yourself up at this late date. Or, more wisely, you can look back upon the person that you were during that period of your life and see that you were probably someone who didn't know as much about yourself or your children as you know today.

People change. We may hold onto certain beliefs and attitudes, but everything else shifts radically. As a young father, I was devoted to my children, but I was also immature. I might lose my temper with them and not give them as much guidance as they needed. Would I do differently today? Of course I would. But did my actions influence my children and make them into substance abusers? Did my own parents make me into the person I am today? I know they did not. I left home at an early age and created my own life. Any problems I've had along the way have been of my own making. I may have been influenced by certain negative experiences during my childhood, but my parents did not "do it to me."

One way of not facing one's own responsibility toward oneself is to go ahead and take the blame head-on. In the same way that addictive children use blame as a way to avoid taking charge of their lives, parents ingest this blame as a way to avoid getting on with theirs.

There are people I know whose parents weren't exactly Ozzie and Harriet, and they were able to rise above their backgrounds. This indicates it isn't always the parent who makes a child take on a negative lifestyle, or a positive one for that matter. More accurately, it is the child who chooses his or her own path. Looking at it this way, parents reading this chapter can at least consider the possibility of not having been such an Almighty influence in their children's lives.

Such a notion may bother some parents. It may also allow other parents to view the situation from a somewhat detached perspective.

Disciplining your children: Could you have done it better?

Kids have to be disciplined, that's just the way it is. It's easy to look back and see yourself as too much of a disciplinarian. Or too little of one. Or someone who used all the wrong methods, such as spanking. Or taking away desserts. Or keeping the child from playing with friends.

Who knows which form of punishment is right? I recall one August day when my kids were seven and eight years old, respectively. I was working in my home office when I heard them outside the door discussing something. Then they came into the room with a proposition.

As my way of disciplining them had been to have them write out "I will not do this" and "I will not do that" lines, a time-consuming chore that kept them away from their friends, they decided that perhaps they could change the scheme of things.

"Instead of giving us lines to write all the time," they asked in unison, "could you . . . just beat us?"

Which just goes to show: Trying to do the right thing doesn't always work.

Two ways of keeping your kids off drugs that probably would work

The first is to go out and find the toughest, meanest-looking ex-wrestler-type and hire him to take care of your kids on a twenty-four-hour basis. Of course, you'll have to come up with a sizeable salary for him plus you'll have to supply room and bath, plus food (and social security), but the rewards will be many. With him on their backs, your kids will have to go to school and do their homework. They won't have a spare moment to inject drugs into their veins and if they don't want to answer to "Bruno," they'll have to respect you.

The second way is to take them very far away where there are no drugs or bad influences. Angela Lansbury did this with her addicted son and it worked. The only thing is, are there any such places on earth today?

What were you like as a child?

To understand the temptations a child faces each day, think back to the time when you were around twelve or thirteen years old. Crack cocaine wasn't around but marijuana, alcohol, and cigarettes were.

Can you honestly say that you, your friends, and your schoolmates totally bypassed these substances?

Even with strict parental guidance, most young-sters experiment with some form of chemical, if for only a short time. You did it; your kids have also done it.

Talking to yourself: Try it

A very good way to start on the road to understand-ing and truth is to interview yourself. Ask yourself a dozen or so questions regarding the way you raised your children.

One of the questions might be: Have I ever intentionally set out to harm my child? Other ques-tions you might ask yourself are:

1. Do I blame myself for the negative actions of my kids?

2. Have I stood in the way of my children's growth by not letting them take the consequences of their actions?

3. Did their actions reflect upon my life and happiness? If they were in trouble did I deny myself a pleasant, peaceful, fulfilling existence? More precisely, did the quality of my life rise and fall according to how my kids were getting on?

4. Do I find a link between the behavioral, attitudi-nal, and addictive traits of my children and their hereditary background? If so, do I blame myself for that—on top of everything else?

5. Do I think I have to suffer because my children

are suffering? Is this a misery-loves-company syndrome?

6. Does thinking this way improve or worsen the situation?

7. Do I really want relief from the problem or does taking on the responsibility of how my kids mismanage their affairs provide a terrific payoff for me?

8. Am I afraid to release the guilt I feel toward my children? Would I have less of a life if I did so? Or, even scarier, *more* of a life?

9. Do I really think I have the power invested in me to influence my children so completely that they do terrible things to themselves? Is there a chance they may be acting on their own in these matters? Without my influence?

10. What would I do with my life if my kids suddenly straightened out the way I think I'd like them to? (This is a frightening thought to some.)

These are just some of the questions that might come up in a good chat with yourself. The answers might turn out surprisingly in favor of your finally abandoning the masochistic tendency to punish yourself over your children.

3

Expectations, and Why It's Dangerous to Have Them

KIMBERLY AND MARK'S STORY. The playroom of Kimberly and Mark's house is your usual jumble of mismatched furniture, TV, stereo, pool table, various oddities strewn around the room or hung on walls, and even a trampoline in the corner. You almost expect a gang of teenagers at any moment to come bounding into the room and flop down on the much-abused couch to watch a football game on TV.

But there are no teenagers here. There *are* random photographs showing one young man, in particular, who bears a striking resemblance to Mark. He has the same thatch of red hair and lopsided grin. This, I take it, is Alex, the nineteen-year-old son whose once-high potential has been destroyed through drug addiction.

Alex is among those former addicts who are rarely brought into the public awareness: the young people who today suffer severe physical and mental disabilities through misadventures with powerful drugs. Some, like Alex, are little more than vegetables who will be institutionalized for the rest of their lives.

I pick up the photo of Alex and ask a few questions about him. At the mention of their son's name, Kimberly and Mark look distressed. It's obvious that while Alex may be out of pain forever, Kimberly and Mark probably won't ever be. My questions lead right to the reason I'm in their house in the first place: to talk about how they've dealt with the tragedy of their son.

But first I ask them what expectations they had for their son before he succumbed to drugs.

"I guess I was over-ambitious for Alex," Kimberly replies. "I came from a very unhappy home and I vowed to myself that my children would have a really loving and nurturing home life and would go on to do fantastic things with their lives. Also, because of health problems, I was only able to have this one child whom I pinned all my hopes on."

"I also pinned a lot on Alex," Mark says. "Today, I'd settle for a child who was just average, but Alex showed amazing brilliance and intelligence. So we applied some pressure by sending him to a special school and so on. There we were, expecting Alex to be a super-achiever. Neither Kimberly or I realized how disturbed he had become after turning thirteen or so. It was around then that Alex got into trouble with some other kids for smoking marijuana in their dorm. As this was his first offense at the school, he was let off with a stiff warning."

"Which apparently meant nothing to Alex," Kimberly interjects. "The next thing we knew, Alex was in trouble again. It was drugs. He was put on probation and warned that one more incident would get him expelled. We didn't know what to do for Alex to get him back on track. We took him to a child psychologist, which didn't help. Then he was expelled, and after that there was the rehab. I really thought he had a chance when he got out of the rehab. But in less than twenty-four hours, he was back on drugs. This was after spending a year at the rehab, doing brilliantly in his schoolwork, and seemingly determined to stay clean once he was out of there. Did you know that sixty percent of all kids coming out of rehabs return to drugs?"

"Then," Mark says, "just before Alex's sixteenth birthday, it happened. From what we've been told, it was some bad crack cocaine—as if there were such a thing as 'good' crack cocaine. We didn't know Mark was using this stuff. But if we'd been paying closer attention, we might've suspected because by this time he was incredibly hostile and off the wall.

School was a thing of the past and he refused to see a doctor. We were pretty much off the wall ourselves from all this going on. Anyway, we were out to dinner with friends one night and when we returned, we found Alex, right there in the playroom, unable to move or respond. He'd thrown up and could've suffocated in his own vomit the way Jimi Hendrix did."

Kimberly and Mark get involved in telling me this story of their son, but then remember that this interview is about them, not him. I ask them how Alex's drug-taking affected their happiness, security, and motivation.

I don't know if this is the first time Kimberly and Mark ever considered such a question, but I can see they're trying to find the right words.

"I just stopped living," Kimberly says. "I just did the essential things, the shopping and the cooking, but otherwise I didn't pursue anything new or pleasurable in my life. As far as I was concerned, if Alex wasn't going to be able to live, then I certainly wouldn't allow myself to live. I felt that were I to go on and be whole, I was somehow betraying a son who could never be whole again."

"I guess you could say the same was true for me," Mark says. "I even felt guilty about having a good relationship with Kimberly. In fact, we split up a few times because of what happened, but we always got back together again, thank God. In terms of work, I started to sabotage what was happening there—being successful made me nervous. I'd had such expectations for my son that I was eaten up emotionally when he threw his life away. I couldn't deal with it."

"That was the hardest part of it for Mark and me," Kimberly says. "Like all parents, we had looked forward to so many things. And then we realized there would be nothing. There'd be no growing into manhood for our son—he'd never graduate high school or attend a prom or have a career. He would just live out the rest of his days in that institution. You know, he looks fine physically—it's just that his brain is gone. When we go to visit, he doesn't recognize us or anything. He just sits there and stares at nothing in particular. As far as we know, he may live to a ripe old age in this condition. Of course, we won't be around. But life goes on. I cry less frequently, but I still cry at the thought of Alex. I grieve for what never was and never can be. I cry for Mark and his pain and I cry for myself. But I think Mark and I are coping as well as can be expected. I realize a lot of life has been forfeited, not just Alex's, but Mark's and my own. I would say that having expectations of one's child is a tenuous thing at best. And these days, with drugs out there and available to such a degree, and with young lives being ruined and families suffering so much, it's incredibly sad. We accept that, unless there is some miracle, Alex will never return to us. He's not dead, but it's like he's dead. And that is just something we have to contend with."

"What we had in mind for Alex was our dream," Mark says. "It had nothing to do with reality. We're in therapy, which is helpful. Kimberly and I have to work out some anger and some resentment toward each other, but we're willing to do it. I don't know, nothing is the way either of us thought it would be. I still have to psyche myself up each day just to get out of bed. For parents who are in the same situation as us, I'd like to say that it's very important not to base your life on what your son or daughter does or doesn't do, achieves or doesn't achieve. Or whether your son or your daughter is hurting him or herself by way of drugs, alcohol, or negative attitude problems. All parents have expectations of their kids— some are realistic, but a great many aren't. Parents wouldn't be human if they didn't have these expectations. However, if parents go under when a child of theirs is hell-bent on self-destruction, they're not only cheating themselves out of the possibility of happiness and contentment, but they're not going to be available to the remaining members of their family—namely, each other as well as their other children who still need them."

Kimberly and Mark's story parallels many other stories I've heard over the years from parents whose high hopes for their youngsters have been dashed. And, of course, it parallels my own.

Three kinds of expectations

As my kids were growing up, I had all three of them.

The first were expectations that my children would grow up achieving many great victories for themselves and that they, as adults, would have all the happiness and professional success they deserved.

Then when drugs entered the picture and I saw my original plan shot down, I had expectations that my children would get back on track and would still be able to enjoy happy, useful lives. I was still confident.

Finally, when I saw this wasn't going to happen either, came the "dangerous" expectations I continued to have, that even after hundreds of disappointments, "this time" it would be different. Of course, it never was. It was as though I simply couldn't learn from experience. Or maybe I just couldn't face the truth. Whatever the case, I was tied into my expectations and was struggling with reality.

I think that these expectations were the true key to my frustration, grief, and disappointment. Had I not had them so strongly, I might have had a more rational view toward remedying this most difficult situation. But then I would have had to surrender all those visions for my children that I had held so close to my heart for so many years. And I obviously wasn't willing to do that.

Most parents I've interviewed have had expectations that their children would excel in school, graduate university (possibly with honors), move into excellent jobs and careers, attract the right mate, and give them beautiful grandchildren. There were also expectations that the children would eventually make lots of money and garner prestigious awards in their particular fields. And, who knows, maybe even help mankind.

Such worthwhile pursuits allow the average parent the security of knowing his or her kids are safe and happy. Safety and happiness, I've discovered, top the list of what most caring parents want for their offspring. To know that a child will eventually land a good job allows them to breathe more freely. When a parent feels that a child isn't happy or even remotely within range of the niceties of life, the worry and tension that a parent undergoes can be cruelly painful. Such is the way of parenthood.

Where did these expectations come from, anyhow?

When my kids were born, I transferred (wrongly) to them many of the dreams and desires I once had for myself. I created for them a lifestyle which I, as a child, would have treasured. My aim was to give them the kind of happy childhood that would support them as they were growing up and, later, as adults. They'd be able to look back and reminisce on their perfect childhoods. I was attempting to set them up to feel good about themselves and to breed self-confidence in them which they could carry forth into adult life. I had expectations that all the love, effort, time, concern, and planning I was pouring into them would eventually pay off, with them turning out to be happy, well-adjusted adults who would feel comfortable in themselves and in the world.

When this desired end didn't materialize and when I saw my kids were doing just the opposite of what I'd envisioned for them, I felt stunning shock and surprise. And yet, throughout all this, I still hung onto those expectations. I just wasn't getting the message. I hadn't owned up to the tragic course my kids were on but more than that, I hadn't owned up to the fact that the expectations I'd had for my kids were the sole property of myself and no one else. As I was to learn over the years, a parent cannot force a child to think his or her way, especially if that child is on substances. My children disclaimed any and all designs I might have had for their lives.

All the guidance, care, and warmth in the world could not have swayed my children off their chosen path. For a brief period during their teen years I still had a certain amount of power over them. I could insist they get therapy, obey household rules and boundaries, and, when their addictions became extreme, enter rehabs. All of these efforts were futile, however. I had expected miracles and found, after years of trying desperately to turn things around, that there had been no progress at all. Instead of getting better, the situation got worse. For example, one of my children was in a rehab. For a while it appeared that he was responding to treatment. But he was out of the rehab for only a few days before he started using again.

If only I had looked at the series of events leading up to our family tragedy with even a semblance of rational thought or detachment, I could have seen that my perspective was based upon what I wanted for my children, rather than what they were willing to do for themselves. In my own youth, I rebelled fiercely against what my father wanted for me—but at least I was willing to work toward reaching my own goals. Of course, times were different then—in school, we still respected our teachers, guns weren't prevalent, drugs weren't on the scene. It was a safer world in which to have dreams.

I saw no curiosity or concern emanating from my children on the subject of their futures. I'd envisioned them attending top universities and studying law or medicine. In those days I was aware of the clock. I was aware that successful young people who move ahead move fast, on a very tight schedule. I visualized my children racing along with confidence, keeping up with and even accelerating past the best of their competitors, receiving the highest scholastic honors and premium professional opportunities.

But much more than that, I wanted them to be

fulfilled, to really enjoy their youths, to get the most from them. I wanted them to have adventures—trekking in the Himalayas, tramping all over Europe, working on the oil lines of Alaska. I wanted them to make quality friends who'd be friends for life. I wanted . . .

What actually transpired is a completely different story. One child dropped out of school at fourteen, unable to do drugs and algebra at the same time. Another child barely made it through high school, but he did make it. This was quite an achievement for him seeing that he was, apparently, also strung out on substances.

My expectations, towering at first, dropped to "Will they make it through college in this condition?" to "Will they make it through their teens?" to "Will they make it through today?"

When expectations don't materialize

At the beginning of their downward spiral, I was a mixture of anger, frustration, and confusion. I didn't know how to handle my kids, myself, or my expectations. The learning curve that would take me from ignorant to informed was still in my future. As for my children, they were oblivious to anything that I was experiencing, drugged as they were.

To liberate myself, I finally had to see things as they really were. I recognized that, much as I wanted to, I couldn't "fix" the situation. I recognized that the simple act of seeing my kids wasting their days and years was a judgment on my part. Somewhere along the line I had confused having helped create my kids with trying to control those creations. Without a doubt they weren't living up to my expectations, but did this make them wrong and me right? There was a distinct possibility that they might not come out of the grasp of their addictions. Would I be able to accept this? Did I have any choice but to accept this?

Whatever the future held, I knew I had to detach completely (or as close to completely as possible) from what my kids were doing. I had to take whatever dreams, aspirations, and expectations I had for my kids and pack them up. Better still, let them go. In coming to terms with the fact that those dreams, aspirations, and expectations belonged to me alone, how could I continue being disappointed in my kids for not fulfilling them?

Having expectations can result in bodily harm

An ongoing problem that created continual unrest at home was my kids' propensity toward violence—much of which was expressed in the form of verbal threats. When I wasn't around, these outbursts were often punctuated by the destruction of furniture and household items. From bright, loving children, they seemed to transform into explosive individuals at puberty—a transformation I originally saw as the passage into adolescence. However, as time went on, I saw that because of the substances they were taking into their bodies, it actually could be dangerous to be around them. It wasn't that I didn't know how to defend myself, it was simply that I didn't feel I could use these defensive measures—some of which I'd learned in the Marine Corps and were quite effective—against my own children.

Is the world safe for parents?

Luckily, I was never put to the test, although I know of many parents who've suffered physical injury from their youngsters. Both mothers and fathers have been severely beaten and hospitalized. And then there are the parents who are murdered by their kids—an increasing phenomenon, as reported on the ten o' clock news and in newspapers.

For several years I lived under the threat of violence. There was tangible evidence of this from time to time, especially when I was vocal over the way they were conducting themselves. More than once I quelled a violent attack by calmly talking one of them down. It was obvious to me that I wasn't so much being threatened by my children as by the influence of drugs and booze upon them.

For most of the survival years that I lived through, and until the time I was able to say "enough" and relinquish my children, I held onto the hope that at any moment they might change,

become normal, act in a positive way, become en-
thusiastic and motivated and respectful of themselves and others. That, of course, never happened.
It just wasn't part of their agenda.

Meanwhile, my marriage fell apart. My wife
couldn't confront her children regarding their addiction, nor could she express her grief or anger in an effective way. The kids clearly disappointed her. If I'd
had certain expectations of our children, she had a
great many more. There had been love, caring, and
guidance coming from her as they were growing up,
but she was unable to deal with the terror that was
now stalking our family. There was only one outlet
for her unhappiness and I became that outlet.

Frustrations can destroy relationships

If parents are unable to work out the causes for their
unhappiness with the parties involved, namely their
problem children, they'll go to the next best source:
each other. Remonstrations of blame will usually be
the order of the day. I read somewhere that when a
child dies, in forty percent of the cases, the parents
separate or divorce within a year. An equally high
percentage of parents split when the expectations
they had for their children don't materialize and the
parents instead experience grief and upset.

So not only can expectations destroy one's
health and career, they can destroy the relationships
of people who might have otherwise spent the rest

of their lives together. Parents who fail to see their partners as their best friends, who fail to support their partners when the going gets rough, probably won't make it through the crisis of a child in trouble. Along the same lines, parents who disagree with the way their partners are handling the crisis will probably sever the relationship.

Expectations play havoc on a parent who is vulnerable to disappointment and its aftermath. I've found that being an "expectations junkie" is akin to having a dread disease. And just like anything else potentially deadly, it can't be wiped out overnight. It has to be understood and treated. When I first realized the seriousness of the problem, I had to take a huge breath and then detach from just about everything my kids were doing—no matter how bad or how good. Bad news was common and always had a devastating effect. But good news could be just as devastating when it eventually turned into bad news again, as it always inevitably did. So I retreated from the problems my children continually manufactured. I decided that if I was to gain any ground toward health, I must allow my children to have those problems and to work them out (or not work them out) themselves.

Suspending judgment—indefinitely

Then came the hard part. I had to end my habit of passing judgment on the way my kids were running their lives. I had to keep an eye on myself and my reactions not just on a daily basis, but on an hourly one as well. There were many slips in the beginning. For example, I could go for a whole day without drowning in sorrow over the way my kids were squandering their lives—and then "lose it" over a phone call with one or the other telling me of some fresh disaster. Many were the days, the weeks, and months like this before I started feeling any relief. Then it started to kick in: an emotional cushioning that could withstand the latest shock. Along with this padding came, for me, the beginning of the end of the expectations syndrome that had kept me in a continual state of paralysis for so many years.

I started to see my children as people in a world of people, acting out their roles. Instead of thinking of them as the young children they had once been, I started seeing them as they were in the present. There wasn't much to indicate they'd ever been those young children. The expectations I'd harbored were associated with them as they were then, not as they are now. As much as it saddened me, I had to admit to myself that those "kids" were gone forever. They had existed for a time and had given me great joy, but there was no trace of them any more. My children were now nearly-grown strangers. I loved them and yet I didn't know them. Nor could I ever know them in the way I had known and related to them as small children.

Even if they hadn't been chemically hooked, it's doubtful I could have known them that way. Children grow up. Sometimes it's many years before their parents do.

I found the transition from being an "obsessed parent with expectations" to "just a parent" the most difficult I'd ever encountered. But once I had made the journey over that long, long bridge, I found a freedom that was extraordinary. This was because the choices my children made for themselves no longer influenced the ones I began to make for myself.

They could drink and drug or get into recovery programs as they chose. I saw this as their decision —without expectations on my part. For parents who haven't yet reached this place of awareness, I can make the following suggestions. I only wish I'd known of them a long time ago.

1. Write out a list of expectations that you have for your children.

2. Read over this list and understand that these are *your* expectations. They have nothing to do with what your children might choose for themselves.

3. Write out a list of expectations that you have for yourself.

4. Read over this list. This is *your* life's work. It has nothing to do with your children.

4

You Did Everything for Your Kids: Maybe You Shouldn't Have

ALICE AND HANK'S STORY. Alice and Hank are somewhere in their mid-to-late seventies. Their house in Stuart, Florida, is in a neighborhood where other elderly people reside. They've been living there for fifteen years, ever since Hank's retirement. They had left Farmingdale, Long Island, and most of their family and friends, but took a golden retriever named Fred (now deceased), a 1966 Ford station wagon (now also deceased), and an alcoholic son they called Denny, short for Dennis.

"We couldn't just leave Denny behind in New York," Alice says in a voice straight out of Brooklyn. She's a frail-looking woman with pure white hair and ankles swollen from the Florida heat, but her spirit seems resilient.

"Why not?" Hank, her husband asks. He acts as if joking, but somehow you know he's not joking.

"Because," Alice starts to answer, "he's never been on his own, that's why."

"It's never too late," Hank says with a humorous flourish. "I mean, who ever heard of a man in his forties living at home with his mommy and daddy?"

"When you're in your forties, *it is* too late," Alice says. "He doesn't know the first thing about living on his own." Alice and Hank seem oblivious of me as they go back and forth with their light bantering. More likely, they're putting on a show for me.

"And what happens if you and I should just so happen to drop dead, Alice?" Hank asks.

"We'll cross that bridge when we come to it," Alice replies.

The squabbling that absorbs Hank and Alice appears good natured enough. Yet I detect something in their demeanor that conjures up extreme sadness and turmoil.

It occurs to me that Denny could walk in on us as we discuss him, but Alice says he's gone out somewhere.

"We're happiest when Denny goes out," Hank says candidly.

"Now, now, Hank,"Alice interrupts, "that's not exactly true although I admit it's partially true. Denny is always so . . . easily riled up about things. Everything that's done for him has to be exactly right or else."

"Or else what?" I ask.

"Or else he's liable to throw a fit," Alice says matter-of-factly.

"What kind of fit?" I ask, pursuing this line of dialogue.

Alice thinks about that before answering. "Well," she finally says, "on one occasion he just about wrecked everything in this room. And another time he put his foot through the television because he didn't think I was listening to what he was saying while it was on. But he'd been drinking heavily that night."

Alice makes this last statement about the drinking casually, as if she wants the idea of it to blend into our conversation only half-heard. But the drinking element sheds a new light on the situation that goes way beyond having a middle-aged son living in the house. This is a middle-aged son with a drinking problem.

"You don't seem very bothered by your son's behavior," I say. "I mean, here you have a forty-two-year-old man living with his parents who are in their seventies, breaking up furniture, and wrecking the TV set. And drinking."

"I didn't say I'm not bothered," Alice says. "We just don't have any answers . . ."

"It's all because you always spoiled him," Hank says suddenly in a tone that says attack.

"I did not," Alice answers.

"You did so," Hank insists. Now I feel I'm in the room with two five-year-olds.

"Maybe I did a little too much for our boy," Alice concedes. "I never pushed him very hard. I made it very comfortable for him to just go on living with us year after year. Maybe I didn't want to let him go."

"Maybe Denny didn't want to let you go," Hank says.

"Has he ever worked?" I ask.

"Oh, yes," Alice says just as Hank answers, "You gotta be kidding!"

"He's been violent toward the furniture and the TV. Has he ever been violent toward either of you?"

This time it's Hank who wants to deny everything. But Alice won't let him.

"He's been violent toward his father. As recently as this week. His father asked him to take out the garbage. The next thing you know he has his father up against the wall, lifting him off his feet by the collar. It's a good thing I was there or Denny might've killed him."

"It was nothing," Hank says, "I should've taken out the garbage myself the way I usually do."

"Does this kind of thing happen often?" I ask, looking at Alice who has tears in her eyes.

"It happens all the time," she says, starting to weep. "Denny has even pushed me around. At one time I would've given him a good smack in the head if he tried anything like that, but now I'm afraid he'll smack me back."

Alice's formerly casual tone is now replaced with one of genuine fear.

"You know you can do something about this . . ." I start to say.

"He'll kill himself," Alice breaks in, knowing what I'm about to suggest. "He told us. If we try to move him out of the house, even to an apartment of his own, or bring anyone in to talk to him—he said he would put a bullet through his brain."

"He has a gun?" I ask, incredulous.

"He has a whole arsenal in his closet—which he keeps locked," Hank says.

It's evident how frightening all this is for Alice and Hank, and there's more.

"And he says he'll take us out with him," Hank continues, "which might be a blessing. We're old and when our time comes, they'll have to put him in some sort of home, I know that. All that stuff I said before about his being on his own is nonsense. He couldn't manage."

I've seen quite a few parents being manipulated this way by their children. I used to be one of them. But this case is doubly sad because what Alice and Hank mistook to be parental love and caring has now turned into an ugly, three-way situation that has two people who should be enjoying their golden years instead nursemaiding a dangerous, forty-two-year-old man with a drinking problem.

"I thought that when I retired," Hank says, "I'd be able to spend my days out on the golf course without a care in the world. But that's impossible. I never know what might happen back here at the house. With Denny's temper, anything could happen. I worry about Alice having to deal with a madman."

"I don't know what we're going to do," Alice says in quiet despair. "I just don't know."

The strong parent

One of my favorite stories is that of Mrs. Buscaglia, the mother of the author and humorist, Leo. Leo tells an account of how his mother tried to talk him out of venturing to Rome with limited funds as a young man. She told him his money wouldn't last and she was, of course, right. When the money ran out so did, according to Leo, all the new friends in Rome he'd been so lavishly spending his money upon. Leo, now broke, thought nothing of wiring his mother for financial assistance. But to his surprise, he got no reply. In desperation, he wired her again, this time a one-word message: Starving! To which she replied with a one-word message of her own: Starve!

From Leo's view, his mother's actions taught

him volumes about taking responsibility for himself. With his mother refusing to "make everything right" for him, he had no choice but to remedy the mess he'd got himself into. And although her lesson seemed harsh at the time, he has come to recognize how extraordinarily wise his mother was and how greatly her ideas on parenthood benefited him.

Letting the child learn

To let a child fall on his or her face is, in my opinion, the most loving gesture a parent can make toward a child. It's also an important part of the guidance the parent owes the child. This doesn't mean that a parent should neglect the child in any way, or even refuse to offer help when necessary. It simply means to learn *when* that offer of help *is* necessary.

When my oldest son was thirteen months old, his brother was born. Up until that moment, the oldest baby had been the only baby. Now there were two of them and the oldest went into a tremendous depression which my wife and I found painful to behold. It was because of our pain in seeing him so unhappy that we overcompensated for him, giving him a bit more time and attention than we gave the new arrival. Thus began a lifelong pattern of catering to our older son which, in retrospect, created sorrows that continue to this day. In essence, what my wife and I had done was to take emotional responsibility for the older boy, thereby cheating him of the knocks and bruises that are part of growing up. As for our younger son whom we loved every bit as much as his older brother, he was also cheated, sacrificed to a certain degree in this unfortunate situation.

It's never too early to teach a child

Being a parent doesn't mean that one knows how to address the growing lessons of one's young. Wisdom often crops up only after the fact. For example, I look back on yet another instance of poor guidance on my part. When the boys were both still very small, we often went to a local park where there were rolling hills. My kids loved to roll down those hills, but they didn't like transporting themselves back up again. They would whine, scream, yell, and holler until I picked them up and carried them to the top, whereupon they would roll down amidst shrieks of laughter—and then the whole process would begin once more.

Were this to happen today I, with my accumulated wisdom, might act as a trainer for my children instead of as a doting father seeking love from his little ones. I might *help* them up the hill instead of carrying them. I might treat them as capable of doing things for themselves, such as negotiating a simple hill. Today, having a far better idea of what works and what doesn't, I might let my small children cry a bit and then struggle a bit while getting up that hill themselves, even if to them the hill looked like Mt. Everest. I think I would have been doing a better job as a parent, and I would have been providing proper guidance. As it turned out, that hill in the park was only one of the many hills in life that I've carried my children up. It's symbolic of the role I chose for myself in my children's lives and the role in which they grew accustomed seeing me.

The road to disaster

Today, as I observe parents with their small children, I can see that many of them are setting themselves up for potential disaster in years to come when those infants and toddlers become teenagers and young adults. They're doing this by being overly protective and by becoming almost fanatical caretakers. They may see themselves as great parents, but what exactly is a great parent? My revised view is that a great parent is one who protects the child from the ills of the outer world, but not always from the rich, varied, and sometimes harsh realities of its inner world.

It seems to be the fashion today for parents, especially fathers, to be totally involved with their children. When I was a kid, my father worked. If I saw him for more than five minutes a day, I counted myself as lucky. For that reason, and because I didn't want my children growing up with an absentee father, I was always available to them. The message very early on for them was that I was a constant fixture, ready to help them in every instance. Because of my decision to become my own boss at a certain point in my career, and because my office was near our home, I was able to take them to school, pick them up, play in the afternoons, and, in general, be a part of their growing-up years. While my father had been at one extreme involvement-wise, I was at the other. I now realize that being too much of a parent—like everything else off balance—can be just as counterproductive as being too little of one.

For one thing, it doesn't allow a child to solve various problems that arise if there's always a big, looming parent to do it for him or her. Traditionally, in former generations, mothers were the ones saddled with the problems associated with the bringing up of children, at least during daylight hours. Fathers, in many families, were like the higher court, approached with problems only when they warranted his precious time. Being on the carpet before one's father meant that a serious misdemeanor had been committed and that swift justice was about to be meted out, usually in the form of privileges denied or a spanking.

In any case, parents were normally far too busy as homekeeper and breadwinner to administer excess attention on their children. Kids in those days had to depend upon their own resourcefulness, intuition, and intelligence in order to get through the scrapes, crises and emergencies (some of which appeared gargantuan) that cropped up on a daily basis. To have a parent that a child could actually "talk to" was still at least a generation away.

How parents have changed

Then, during the 1960s, something happened which changed the way parents would relate to their children from that time on. That "something" was the free-love/hippie/gender-role revolution that took place in various parts of the globe. Suddenly, it was okay for mothers and fathers to let down their guards and step out of their gender roles. It was socially acceptable to become pals with one's kids. Thus began the democratized family unit, with the child having a voice and a vote. The old adage that "children should be seen and not heard" used by generations to keep kids "in their place," was now made obsolete by parents who subscribed to new ways of child-rearing. As far as *these* parents were concerned, anything had to be better than the way they were brought up.

The all-powerful parent voluntarily downsized his or her role in the family governing system and allowed the child greater freedom of self-expression. Many women coming into motherhood created innovative ways to "reason" with their children in place of the methods of control and coercion used by their parents. Fathers were given permission to become more visible in the upbringing of their children. They could even take on a nurturing role, formerly the exclusive preserve of the mother. To see a man pushing a baby carriage in the 1950s was rare. By the 1970s, the sight of a father pushing his child along in a stroller had become common. Just as common became the presence of the father in the delivery room. This was quite a departure from the stereotypical, chain-smoking, floor-pacing, dad-to-be who used to sweat it out in the waiting room!

I was one of those fathers who went into the delivery room. Possibly because of this, I felt a special bonding with my children. It was the start of a "giving" pattern directed toward my children from their very first minutes out of the womb. I was giving of myself, sharing the experience of their entry into the world, "being there" for them.

Giving to my children, doing things for them, being there for them—these were all phrases in my own personal lexicon of parenthood. I wanted to give them the best possible lives and was willing to do anything it took to reach that end. Additionally, I would always be there helping them, guiding them, lovingly showing them the way.

This was a neat little plan of mine. But it didn't leave much room for them contributing to, or being there for, themselves.

The training I'd received as a child in learning to become self-sufficient was in the school of hard knocks: without the aid and support of parents, family, teachers, counselors, or child psychologists. It had been pretty tough learning the ways of the world without the benefit of concerned adults. So when my children arrived, I didn't want them to have to cope the way I'd had to. As a result, my wife (whose philosophy at this juncture was identical to mine) and I took on the task of keeping the real world away from our kids. In doing this, we inadvertently deprived them of valuable growth and learning skills. This put them into a position (which became a habit) of depending upon us. My wife and I became the "doers" for our children. We became human shields, positioning ourselves between our kids and just about everything and everyone they came into contact with.

For example, if they had even the slightest problem at school, my wife and I would exhaust ourselves looking for solutions. If they were being harassed by schoolmates, we might talk to their parents. If they had a failing grade, we'd whisk them off to a tutor. Whatever came up for them, they knew we'd handle it. They could approach me with a problem anytime, even call me at work. Later on, phone calls from my kids were replaced by phone calls from school officials, police, or drug counselors. They were contacting me in connection with my children, and of course that took precedence over my work. Whenever talking to authorities, I was left feeling drained. I was fighting a battle for my children that I couldn't win.

Getting out of the way

Had I just stepped aside and let nature take its course, I would have done my entire family a service. But I was so caught up in this "doing" pattern that it never occurred to me to simply let go. If one or both of my sons had to appear in court because of an offense they had committed (such as drunk driving), I was right there with a lawyer and a check to cover the fine. Had I not attempted to save my kids from the clutches of the law, the boys would've had to pay the consequences of their actions themselves, with either jail time or community service or both. But what parent *won't* try to keep his or her child out of jail?

The answer to that is the parent who is *aware,* who has learned from experience that it's better to let one's children do the same. Nothing teaches a child or serves a child as well as learning from the mistakes that child makes.

By continually bailing my kids out of unpleasant situations which they'd created, I was, in effect, telling them that they didn't have to adhere to laws, rules, or boundaries of any kind. They could do whatever they wanted, spread mayhem wherever and whenever they wanted. After all, they had parents who'd fix it for them, pay their fines, talk to the authorities, get them out of jam after jam.

There is no reason why they should have thought differently. I had established a dynamic in their early days which essentially took them off the hook whenever they did anything against society. This is not to say that their mother and I hadn't tried to teach them the difference between right and wrong. We admonished them privately, but we couldn't let them pay publicly. We'd talk to them, try to make them see how negative their actions were. I also made some extremely foolish mistakes when it came to punishing them, the biggest of which was in not carrying through the sentence. In other words, I might refuse one or the other the use of the car and then, a little while later, relent because I felt sorry for him. It's no wonder these boys felt comfortable creating havoc. They knew their punishment would consist of a verbal telling-off and little else.

By the time my children were in their mid-teens, they had grown stronger and more independent. All forms of punishment became obsolete. There wouldn't have been any way to enforce any type of restriction. This was when my wife and I became trapped in a house with two young demons. They could drink and drug as much as they liked and would shrug off the frequent interference they were getting from us. And all the while my policy hadn't changed when it came to rescuing them from police actions. I was right there in the court coughing up the money it took to set them free.

Then, on a cold October day, this pattern was changed for me by a county court judge. He had grown tired of seeing the face of my youngest son before him so often, and he decided that it was time something was done. For driving without a license while under the influence of drugs, my son was remanded to a nearby rehabilitation center for eighteen months.

It took a judge to change the course of events governing our family, and to teach me the value of boundaries.

5

Setting Boundaries and Sticking with Them

DOROTHY'S STORY. The phone rings shortly before midnight. Even before I pick up the receiver, I know it's going to be Dorothy, someone I befriended in a parents support group. And it is. As usual, she's distraught. This is nothing new, she's almost always distraught. The reason she's living in such a high state of anxiety is because she has allowed herself to become a dangling marionette—with her unemployed thirty-three-year-old drug-addicted and abusive son, Tom, acting as the puppet master.

"I just got off the phone with Tom," she says, her voice trembling. "He called me in another one of his drugged, ugly moods demanding money. When I told him I didn't have it to give to him, he started calling me names—like bitch and whore, and a lot worse. Then he was yelling at the top of his lungs that he was going to break into the house one night and slit my throat."

Dorothy, a widow who lives with her boyfriend, is a battle-scarred veteran of these repellent confrontations with this drug-crazed, almost psychopathic son. But regardless of the frequency and the grinding sameness of the content, she never gets used to them: They always leave her shaking like a leaf. Her "policy," for want of a better word, through all these encounters has been to let Tom rant on and on without saying anything much in reply so as to, in her words, "not to add fuel to the fire." But this time, she tells me, there has been a difference in the way in which she reacted.

"I don't know what got into me. I suddenly saw red and I blew my top. I told him I didn't deserve to be treated this way, that I was his mother and that there was no way he'd ever get another cent out of me, and that I had no intention of seeing him or talking to him until he'd been through a drug rehab and was capable of acting like a normal, decent human being. Then I slammed the phone down on him good and hard," she says with seeming satisfaction.

I congratulate Dorothy on the way she's put an end to his pushing her around. Only, suddenly, Dorothy isn't hearing me. As a woman who has never been even remotely assertive with her son before, she is now abruptly overcome with regret over what she has said to him. Her sudden transformation from outspoken mother to crumbling wreck takes place in just a few seconds, but it is total.

"I can't believe I said all that to him," Dorothy moans and begins sobbing. "I can't believe I cut him off like that. I'm his mother, the only person the poor kid has in the world. I feel like I've told him to go straight to hell."

I ask her how many times he's told her the same thing, not just in words, but actions.

"I know, I know," she answers hurriedly over-looking the truth. "But that doesn't give me the right to turn around and say it back to him."

"Why not?" I ask. "This guy has stolen from you, destroyed your home, bled you dry financially to support his drug habit, and you're the one feeling guilty?"

This isn't what Dorothy wants to hear. She has called me a great many times recently and I've always allowed her to ramble on about this particular son; she wasn't calling for suggestions on how to end the misery, but rather just to have someone hear her problems. I was always aware that Dorothy wanted nothing more out of these long phone sessions than to go over and over how terrible it was, how tragic it was. Like a lot of people who'd rather talk about a crippling relationship than do something about it, Dorothy had become an energy vampire. I had to be on guard constantly so that she didn't drain mine.

Any suggestions I might offer her would fall on deaf ears. And anyway, who was I to give advice? I had been in just as bad shape with my own kids until I'd finally pulled out of my slump. But now it looked as if she had taken the first step toward pulling out of hers, a step that would lead her to some sort of sanity in an insane situation. *If she just didn't falter.* That was the key. She had fought back instead of letting the enemy (the drugs in her son's mind, body, and soul) walk all over her. The statement she made to her son couldn't have been clearer: She would have nothing more to do with him until he was drug-free. If only Dorothy could stick to what she'd said.

Her next words to me, however, arouse my frustration: "Do you think I should call him and apologize?" she asks lamely.

Even though I know it's a futile effort, I try to encourage her not to. I may as well be talking to the wall.

"Yes, but what if he kills himself?" she cries out.

I tell her he's already killing himself with his drugs and that, by being so submissive, she's contributing far more to the situation than he is.

She's not ready for this. I understand exactly where she's coming from. I was there myself, as unhearing then as she is now, unable to see how destructive I was being by simply being a wimp. Like Dorothy, I'd been scared to death that if I made any ultimatums with my own addicted kids I would be letting them down, not supporting them, not *being there* for them.

Talking Dorothy out of calling her son is like talking a determined suicide down off a window ledge. It's hopeless. She is calm now, cheerful, unhearing, anxious to cease our conversation. She promises me that she definitely will not call Tom, no matter what happens. But of course I know that she will. The moment she hangs up from me.

An introduction to setting boundaries

Setting boundaries is the first and most important step you can take in changing the dynamics of an unrelentingly harsh parent/addict relationship. It's the surest way parents can gain control over what is essentially a no-win situation. And also attain peace of mind. Setting a boundary is in no way cutting off relations with the child on drugs. *It's cutting off relations with the drugs themselves.*

What might make it easier for parents reading this is to know that their kids are *not* the chemicals they're ingesting. Chemical addiction is recognized by the World Health Organization as a disease over which addicts have little or no control. By the insidious nature of this disease, extreme personality changes are created in a person.

A profile on drug users and alcoholics shows them to be highly sensitive and vulnerable by nature, unable to deal with the chemicals they are putting into their bodies. Unfortunately, even when clean of chemicals, addicts don't always revert back to their normal personalities. They can, and often do, exhibit some of the same tendencies as when they were using. This is known in Alcoholics Anonymous and Narcotics Anonymous circles as being a "dry drunk." But at least they're more rational and less prone to violent behavior.

The only control parents have is over their own actions and reactions. How you deal with your emotions makes all the difference. You can continue to be a victim to what is essentially an insane situation due to the chemicals your children are using, or you can control the situation through the setting of boundaries, making a conscious effort not to allow your addicts to intrude upon you.

What *is* a boundary?

Think of it as a border crossing with sentry posts created and guarded by the parent, a clearly defined barrier which prevents the addict from bringing disorder into the parent's domain. For example, a parent may have to inform an addict who has been removed from the house that he or she cannot be allowed back home unless chemically clean. This action, when enforced effectively, renders the addict powerless over the parent.

Yet, because of the many emotional aspects

involved, creating boundaries with chemically-addicted children remains one of the most difficult and complicated steps parents can take.

The main problem parents face in setting boundaries has to do with the very nature of such a move. When placing a barrier between parent and child, a perception of loss is created. It doesn't matter that the loss may consist mainly of the grief and sorrow indicative of such a relationship—it is still loss. But sometimes grief and sorrow are the only things a parent feels entitled to.

Why parents of addicts don't set boundaries

There are lots of other reasons parents may not choose, or feel themselves capable of, the setting of healthy boundaries with their addicted children. Here are some of them.

Suicide threats. There is the enormous fear on the part of parents that the addict will kill him or herself. Isn't that what the addict is always threatening?

A threat is, according to Webster's dictionary, "an expression of the intention to hurt or punish another." Telling the parent that he or she is going to jump off a bridge or take a lethal overdose is a form of intimidation: It's the ultimate source of power which addicts hold over the heads of their parents and it goes a long, long way. Parents will do anything just as long as the addict doesn't take that final, fatal step.

Addicts have only to *mention* the word suicide

and they've got their parents right where they want them, in the palm of their hand—and they won't hesitate to squeeze.

Fear of never seeing the addict again. This is the exaggerated fear on the part of parents that the addict will disappear, vanish into thin air, once it appears the parent can no longer be manipulated as before. Not knowing the whereabouts or the physical state of one's addicted child can be far more agonizing than actually dealing with the addict's problems.

The vision of the child overdosing and lying dead in a ditch somewhere haunts many parents. At least by having contact, grueling as that contact may be, the parent knows the addict is still alive. And where there's life, there's hope.

A note of reassurance: As a rule, addicts don't disappear permanently. They might stay away for days, even weeks. But they resurface regularly to ascertain whether their disappearing act has sufficiently scared the parents into relinquishing the controls they've set up. These disappearances, which leave many parents in a frantic state of mind, have a marked touch of sadism about them.

Fear of the addict living on the streets. While under the influence of drugs or alcohol, an addict usually doesn't care about such things as sheets on the bed. Living on the streets is, for the addict, a sort of camping out—only in a zonked state. Parents who can't bear the thought of their children stretched out on cold concrete in some alley somewhere strictly avoid setting up boundaries in the home.

Fear of the addict turning to prostitution. Some parents feel that if they don't supply the addict with funds, the addict will get them another way. *Any* other way, prostitution being at the top of the list. Aside from the moral considerations parents may have in terms of their children turning to prostitution, there's the fear of AIDS which strikes a large number of children who sell their bodies.

Parents punishing themselves. Some parents have a deep-rooted conviction that living a life in turmoil is all that they deserve. They rationalize that if they had put more love, time, care, planning, and guidance into the bringing up of their kids, they wouldn't have to contend with this horrific situation today.

Parents who are extremely critical of the job they've done raising their children are apt to accept the idea that they must suffer eternally, that the misery they feel is justified. This lack of self-love and self-esteem very nicely complements the massive burden of guilt such parents carry around with them at all times.

Reluctance to take charge. Sometimes, facing a gruesome family problem—such as the drug addiction or alcoholism of a child—is easier than pursuing a successful career and a meaningful relationship, and also easier than realizing certain goals or allowing for happiness and fulfillment. After all, being totally consumed by the problems of an addict takes every waking minute of the day and night, especially if that addict is your son or daughter.

Doesn't leave much time for you, does it?

Fear of being left behind. There's a fear that the addict will get on with his or her life. Believe it or not—and as bizarre as it sounds—some parents unconsciously dread the possibility of their children succeeding in life, getting ahead, becoming more prosperous, more influential, moving into spheres into which the parent isn't invited. These parents feel their children will leave them behind in the wake of new-found independence and accomplishments. Significantly, they fear they will no longer be needed.

Most parents in this category strenuously deny that they would rather have crippled, addicted children who will never leave them than healthy, successful ones who might. But by continuing to feed the chaos of their addicted children, without even the hint of a boundary, there is little or no chance either party will escape the life-and-death stranglehold they have on one another.

Blaming it on bad genes. There's the theory that drug addiction and alcoholism are hereditary afflictions. To a certain type parent's way of thinking, this theory makes him or her the direct link to the child's having become a drug abuser or an alcoholic.

Using this unfortunate situation as a rationale, the guilt-ridden parent might not think it fair that the child should suffer alone. Many parents who regard their own genes as the cause for the addictions of their young wouldn't dream of creating boundaries. To place restrictions on the addict's behavior and then to move ahead and have a wonderful, happy life is unthinkable.

Their verdict: only the most selfish, unfeeling parents would consider their own well-being over that of their children at such a time.

Abandonment issues. There's the fear that setting up boundaries might give addicted children the idea that they are being abandoned in their greatest hour of need. Again, only the most selfish, unfeeling parents would do such a thing.

The tender trap. The "tender trap syndrome" is a dangerous parental disorder which affects the sight and other senses, and centers around one's offspring. This is where the parent remains stuck in the time when his or her kids were needy and vulnerable infants. That memory, with all its attendant emotional feelings, can persist, even when the kids have grown into adulthood. And it persists even when the kids have become out-and-out addicts. The parent, still protective, cannot re-adjust his or her thinking in order to create restraints.

Pleasing the addict. This one comes out of left field, but there is a bona fide reason behind it, and that's the fear that the addict "wouldn't like it." This is enough for many parents to steer clear of boundaries of any kind.

When I was at the height of the madness with my addicted kids, the idea of setting boundaries never even entered my consciousness. This concept, when I first heard it, seemed to come from another planet. What? Place a wedge between me and my children? Forget it. They could call me at 3 A.M. in an off-the-wall drugged stupor and I would actually try to *reason* with them.

It usually took me a week to ten days to recover from one of these painful encounters. But because I was a parent who had to "be there" for his kids no matter what, I would overlook the late hour, the slurring of their speech, even the obscenities and abuse they would inevitably hurl my way. I was like a twenty-four-hour city dump. By my acquiescence, my kids felt comfortable dumping anything and everything right in my lap. This consisted of all the maniacal, paranoid excesses created by the drugs they were taking. In an extremely sick way, I felt that this was what "being close" to my children was all about. I had some sort of weird belief that the family that goes through hell together is just swell together.

It was through much-needed counseling that I

finally realized that I was playing a major role, most
certainly the pivotal role, in this situation. During
my first session, the counselor sat in a state of dis-
belief as I described the kind of relationship I was
enduring with my kids. If he had been amazed by
this nonchalant portrayal of terror I was painting for
him, I was equally surprised by the force of his reaction. He found it inconceivable that I had allowed
myself to become a virtual punching bag for my
children.

I hadn't understood his reaction at first because,
like a lot of parents, it had never occurred to me
that I wasn't *supposed* to be a punching bag for my
children. I'm not sure just where I'd picked up my
parent-as-victim identity. But as this particular
counselor pointed out, I never would have invited
this kind of mistreatment from anyone else—
friends, co-workers, or even other relatives. But regarding my kids, I had thought nothing of giving
them *carte blanche.*

Once I realized the enormity of the problems
within my family structure and the part I'd played
in bringing them about by being such a "wimp," I
was able to understand that I had to remedy the
situation by strengthening my position—or at least
let it be known that the "wimp" days were over.
Without my active participation in a passive, parent-as-victim role, the dynamics of our interactions

would have to change. Through further counseling, I took the necessary steps to right the wrongs I had created for myself and my family.

The first thing I did was to put a stop to the early morning calls by simply not picking up the phone. This angered the addicts to the extreme, an anger they took out on my answering machine. The fact that I was suddenly not available to them at all times, day or night, was totally unbelievable to them. After all, we had a contract: They would dole out the abuse and I would take it. That contract was now obsolete.

At this point in the proceedings I wasn't cutting myself off from the addicts. I was simply conveying a message to them that I would no longer be there for them to unleash their drugged anger in my direction whenever they wished. This new tone of mine maddened them, but not nearly as much as when I started informing them that their behavior was "inappropriate" (a term I picked up from my counselor). I repeated these words to them every time they'd start flinging insults at me. It took a long time and a great deal of patience and control on my part, but eventually they learned that it was not okay for them to act inappropriately toward me. They knew that if they did so, I would firmly replace the receiver. I also let them know that they would only be able to reach me during normal waking hours—another inconvenience, seeing as my normal waking hours and their normal waking hours were completely opposite.

The fact that I finally, and for the first time since they'd started taking drugs, began disallowing their habit of calling me vicious four-letter names, threatening my life, and demanding large sums of money came as an enormous shock to them. And when I failed to inform them I was taking a two-week vacation in Hawaii, a vacation suggested by my counselor, all hell broke loose on my telephone lines, as I could tell, again, by the demonic messages they left.

It's never too late to draw the line

Once I got the swing of incorporating boundaries into my life and that of my addicted kids, it became a relatively easy thing to maintain. I had never done it before, a mistake I could trace directly to my lack of know-how as a young parent. (It's okay to admit I didn't know everything there was to know as a parent.) When my kids were young and got into trouble, punishments were prescribed but rarely put into effect. This set a very bad standard. The ultimate message this gave them was that I wasn't going to make them take responsibility for their actions. They knew they'd be pardoned and freed, to go out and get into even more mischief for which they, again, wouldn't have to answer. So the act of suddenly introducing them to boundaries when they were in their mid-to-late teens came as a major jolt.

Boundaries: They work both ways

Having embarked on a plan to remedy the situation, I was not the same person any more and the addicts didn't know how to relate to me. When I did speak to them, my whole focus was changed. No longer did I try to persuade them to give up drugs or get jobs or go to school. I was officially and permanently off that program. A big part of creating boundaries —and this is essential to anyone attempting to do such a thing—is to *stop interfering* with what's happening on the other side of the line.

My job, now that I had reclassified myself, was merely to listen, as long as there was no verbal abuse, and to take care of my own needs. This meant that I had to say no to all unreasonable requests: the borrowing of money, the co-signing for a car, bailing them out of problems with the law, and so on.

There are three things to remember in setting up boundaries that work.

1. There are two clearly defined sides to every boundary. On one side of that line is the parent and everything pertaining to the parent. On the other side of the line is the addict and everything pertaining to the addict.

2. Neither party has to know or like what is happening on the other side of the boundary. Neither

party has to approve of anything going on there. The whole idea of the boundary is to separate people and their opinions from one another—to separate likes and dislikes, beliefs, opinions, and behaviors.

3. There can be no contact between parties if the influence of drugs or alcohol makes it impossible to communicate with mutual respect.

Tools required to maintain an effective boundary

There are only two: detachment and an ability to take the drama out of every little occurrence.

The first tool, detachment, is something you have to work on to perfect it for yourself. True detachment has to do with how you're feeling within. In other words, are you really willing to let others live their own lives without your interference or judgment? Or are you just going through the motions? Is your facade one of calm while your inner self is anything but?

How does a parent detach? By understanding that there is nothing the parent can do to change the behavior of the addict. A good way to do this is through meditation, which helps you to build up and maintain a strong sense of peace and harmony within yourself. Meditation has been designated by some doctors as the number one way to reduce stress and, subsequently, the threat of illness. Meditation allows you to let go of the situation and to see that your main job is to take care of yourself so that you don't also fall by the wayside. By taking care of yourself, you are taking a large step toward diminishing the destruction wrought by the attitudes and actions of the addict. Twenty minutes a day, reserved just for you, increases your energy and when your energy is high, things bother you less.

Having a sense of humor in a situation that isn't necessarily funny can lighten the tension of what's going on. By trying not to take every little thing seriously, you will greatly reduce stress. There is a lot of drama associated with drug and alcohol addiction. If you can begin to see how ridiculous most of it is, you can start to put things into perspective.

If you can just laugh and then hang up when the addict calls saying he wants you to bail him out of jail, you've graduated to a new level.

Venturing back over the line

Parents make a big mistake just at the moment when things look like they're improving. They let down their guard. They either slacken up on the conditions governing each boundary, or they give them up altogether, viewing the boundary as having been a temporary measure, no longer applicable once a certain amount of sanity has been achieved.

A word of warning to all parents of drug addicts: DON'T.

To revert to wimpish behavior will land the

parent, the addict, and the entire family right back in the same old mess. A parent's new-found strengths must be preserved at all costs because it is only through these strengths that a family can continue to heal.

Though the addict may not seem to approve of the barrier, this is not always the case. Addicts actually respond to strength. In many ways, they want the parent to create higher standards so that the family can operate successfully. But in other ways, the addict is ever on the lookout for the break in the armor. He or she may have surrendered the kingdom once before, but any opportunity to recapture old ground and wrest back the power from the parent will be acted upon.

Chaos, dissension, and despair—trademarks of the addict—can flare up in an instant. Keeping them at bay is a twenty-four-hour job. So once you've set boundaries, stick to them.

Advanced techniques in setting boundaries

Embellishing on boundaries is possible. The only time my addicted kids ever called me was when they wanted something from me. After I created boundaries, it occurred to me that perhaps, as part of the package, it was up to me to let them know that I was also a person with certain needs of my own. I had a need to be called on my birthday just as

I called them on theirs, and a need to be asked how I was just as I asked them how they were. Incorporating a proper parlance is an important phase in the building of boundaries.

I also made it known to my addicted children that if we were to continue having conversations then it would have to be a two-way street, with them being as thoughtful and considerate toward me as I was toward them. I made it known that I wasn't there simply for the asking of money. This line of reasoning met with derision at first. But when the addicts saw that I was serious about it, and that no conversation could continue without certain civilities, they began to relent. I wasn't asking for anything more than common courtesy. Or should I say, demanding it?

6

Saying Good-bye to the Addicted Child

STACY AND MIKE'S STORY. There are ten or twelve parents sitting in a circle listening to a woman speak. Her name is Stacy. She has trouble getting the words out and seems to be on the verge of crying. What she has to do is odious to her, yet necessary if she wants to survive. Those of us sitting in the circle understand exactly what she's feeling. We've all been there ourselves. The woman's husband, Mike, a burly truck driver, sits next to her looking down at the floor as she speaks. He also appears to be in a state of shock as Stacy asks the group to support them in removing Emma, their drugged-out, eighteen-year-old daughter, from their home. It's also quite apparent that this isn't simply an eviction situation: By putting this person out of the house, her parents are actually saying good-bye to her for all time.

The meeting we're holding in the local town hall is called Tough Love (and, of course, none of the names mentioned are the real ones). This is one of perhaps thousands of parents support groups that are held across the country each week. Parents come here for help and guidance because they know they'll be in the company of other parents who have had or are currently having the same harrowing experiences as they. They know they'll get the kind of help they can't get elsewhere from people who understand exactly what they're going through.

Each person sitting in the circle tonight is a parent who has come to the final, and formerly unthinkable, realization that the relationship with his or her drug-addicted child has drawn to an end. In most cases, permanently.

Stacy explains how she and Mike have reached this same conclusion. "We have tried everything possible to help our daughter, but we see that we have no daughter left. She's an incurable drug addict who will do anything she can to have her drugs."

"We realize this is a medical problem," Mike adds. "But there is no medicine on earth to give us back our little girl. She's long gone. What we have in her place is a person with only one thing on her brain, to stick a needle in her arm. She's out to kill herself and take us along with her. And she has just about succeeded."

Mike speaks these words not out of anger, or even remorse, but out of resignation. "Right now, either Emma goes or we go. In the last five years, we had her in a rehab a half dozen times. Every time she came out, she went right back on drugs again. And once Emma gets hooked again, that's it. She lies to us, rips us off by taking anything she can get her hands on, and is violent toward her mother. If she can't find any money in the house, she'll grab something, anything—a TV, stereo, or whatever—and sell those things to get money for drugs. I can tell you we don't have much left for her to steal."

"This morning was the final straw," Stacy says. "I tried to stop her from leaving the house with a valuable coin collection left to Mike by his grandfather. She knocked me down and took it anyway. I called the police right after she left and reported her taking the coin collection as a robbery. The cops picked her up on the road before she had a chance to sell the coins and brought her back home. In a way, it would have been better if she had tried to sell the collection because then at least I could have had her arrested and detoxed. It's a horrible thing to say, but I feel a lot better when she's behind bars. I feel she's safer, we're safer. It's about the only time I'm able to sleep at night."

The other parents in the circle recognize the truth in this statement. We've all experienced numerous occasions when the only way we could breathe easily was by knowing our children had been temporarily, or, in some cases, even permanently, detained. For parents willing to see their children behind bars, this has to be the ultimate end of uncertainty. And almost glaringly absent from this room tonight is any sign of nagging uncertainty, of hopes and expectations that our children will suddenly recover from their substance habits, begin to lead normal, responsible lives, make everyone proud.

Like Stacy and Mike, many of us in these rooms have called upon the wisdom and experience of fellow members for the task of liberating ourselves, at least physically, from our addicted children. There is a certain form to the procedure. The parent is instructed to find another place for the addict to live, given that the addict is of legal age. The length of notice to be given is one week. On each day of that week, the parent is instructed to inform the addict of the number of days left before the move is to take place. The addict usually ignores what the parent is saying and carries on along his or her destructive path. Finally, on the designated day, the addict is told to be packed because it's time to move.

Should the addict resist, as many do, with the words "You can't force me out of here," parents are instructed to explain that all they have to do is pick up the phone and get help in enforcing the move. Addicts, upon hearing this, usually go peacefully because the last thing they want is a group of their parents' supporters pouncing on them. It's at this time, as they see their children leave, that parents must do what they never thought possible: They must harden their hearts.

Stacy and Mike ask for this kind of assistance from us and we all agree to be on hand if they need us to help them remove Emma from their house and, ostensibly, from their lives.

"I never thought it would come to this," Stacy says, suddenly sobbing into her handkerchief.

"Me, either," Mike agrees. "What have things come to in this world when it's either you or your child?"

How to know when to make the split

To say "you'll know" when to sever physical ties with an addict is taking for granted that you, as a parent, will see past the emotional ties that bind you.

Here's a list of possible reasons to make arrangements for your addict to live apart from you. You don't have to check them *all* off to know.

The addict is violent. This is the number one reason for calling a halt to your addict's living with you. If you fear for your safety or that of other family members—or worse, if there's been actual physical abuse—you are only inviting more of the same by keeping the addict under your roof.

Stress. Because of your addict's behavior and the stress coming from it, you're spending more time at the doctor's office. You've increased the dosage of your anti-depression medicine. You're prone to fatigue and headaches like never before. You're feeling suicidal much of the time.

Your property is destroyed. Your addict has destroyed your property either while in or while out of a drugged state. Smashing dishes against a wall, driving a fist through a wall (from a consensus of parents, this seems to be a favorite), kicking doors in (another favorite) are some examples. Worst-case scenarios extend from flooding the house by leaving the taps on to burning the house down.

Your property is stolen. To finance the purchase of drugs and alcohol, an addict looks in the obvious place for quick cash: your home. If actual cash isn't available, perhaps your checkbook or credit cards will be. Don't rely on banks not to cash forged checks, they do it all the time. And beware of leaving around valuable antiques, heirlooms, or even appliances—anything that can be carted off and hocked. As for stocks and money markets, addicts can be extraordinarily ingenious and knowledgeable when it comes to cashing them in. Chances are you won't even know they've been cashed in for months to come. There have been many cases like these. Some parents have even discovered that their life savings have been converted into fine, white powder.

The addict as a bad influence. Addicts love stoned company and often prey on their younger brothers and sisters. Recruitment begins with a sampling of a drug and can lead to full-fledged addiction and a lifetime journey on the wrong track for the addict's siblings.

You can't take the addict's lies. Addicts are generally incapable of telling the truth. Perhaps you believed that your addict was going to school every day, but then you found out from the school's administrative offices that he or she hasn't been there in a month. Addicts think nothing of lying to their parents (and to anyone else, for that matter). They do it so convincingly that parents instantly forget all the other lies they've been told. "Do you promise me that you will never take drugs again?" a parent might ask the addict. "Of course," the addict will state with a look of utmost sincerity: "What do you think I am, a loser? I've been off that stuff for six months." Sound familiar?

You're facing financial disaster. Your financial life is a nightmare due to the many expenses brought about by the addict. You've bailed him or her out of trouble for years, but who's there to bail you out?

The addict won't go into recovery. You've made endless attempts for your addict to get help—to no avail. And you know that as long as you provide a roof, the addict will make no effort to straighten out on his or her own.

Is this just a convenient excuse to throw your kid away?

When your son or daughter is an inveterate substance abuser without even the slightest intention of going into a recovery program, you are not throwing the person away. You are removing the poisonous aftermath which is a threat to your own life and well-being.

Some parents are so steeped in the quagmire that they can't differentiate between the child they love and the chemical dependency that they don't. To them, their child is their child no matter what happens.

It's only after parents realize that by not changing the course of events, the struggle with the addict will become a fight to the death.

If your addicted child is of legal age and avoiding a recovery program, you owe it to yourself, and the addict, to make your home off limits.

Don't try to evict the child on your own

The task of removing a child from one's home is no fun for anybody. It seems contrary to every instinct in the parent's being. But the alternative, letting the addict feed off the parent, is infinitely worse for all concerned. To successfully carry out a plan to separate from the child, the parent needs the support of other parents who've made the break.

The best place to find these other parents are in the rooms of Tough Love, Al-Anon, Nar-Anon, and Parents Anonymous. The heavy burden parents of addicts carry is lifted by the compassion and understanding found in these support groups.

To find that one is not alone in one's grief, and that the problems facing parents of addicts are far more common than one thought, is a source of strength. Asking for advice from other parents who've taken steps to liberate themselves, and allowing those parents to assist you in achieving your goal, is the best way to make the transition. This help is never volunteered; it has to be asked for.

Liberation from your addict: the pros

Once the arrangements are made and carried out, most parents who have physically separated themselves from their addicted children will feel astonishing relief. Not having the continuous stress associated with being around a dedicatedly disruptive and destructive person is extremely refreshing. You and the other members of your family feel the change in the atmosphere almost immediately.

Arranging for the addict to live elsewhere gives you time to get a better perspective on the situation and to build up your seriously depleted emotional reserves.

On the health front, you'll notice that by taking yourself out of the addict's radius of manipulation you will have given yourself a total and much-needed physical and mental uplift.

No longer will you have to be on your guard all the time, steeling yourself for the daily grind of defeatism so associated with drug addicts and alcoholics.

Relationships that you've put on hold in order to cater to the addict—such as those with your spouse and other children—can be resumed. There is now time to repair those relationships that might have been hurt through your neglect.

Valuables won't have to be locked away. You can go back to your former practice of leaving the TV in the living room and your jewelry in your jewel box. Without worrying about it.

You won't be living in fear of the addict's gut-wrenching "surprises" awaiting you on a daily basis.

You won't have to tiptoe around or watch your every word in the presence of the addict in order to prevent violent reactions on his or her part.

And finally, you'll be able to pursue those career goals and pastimes for which you had no time or energy while the addict was busy violating all the basic tenets of a normal home life.

Liberation from your addict: the pitfalls

Liberation is sweet but it can be short-lived. What often follows the forcing of an addictive child out of one's home is an overpowering feeling of guilt and fear. Guilt because of what the parent had to do—and did—and fear because the parent has no idea how the addict may be faring.

The stress that the addict created for the parent by being in close proximity is soon replaced by the stress the parent now creates for him or herself through self-imposed agonies of guilt and fear. Weighing the two alternatives, the parent is often left with the feeling that having the addict living away is worse than having the addict live at home.

It's at just about this time that the remorseful parent gets in the car and brings the addict home again. Sometimes after just a few hours' separation.

Any good which might have come from the expulsion is now forever canceled and the parent's credibility is seriously diminished. Even if there are conditions to which the addict agreed in order to be reinstated in the home, events of the past show that an addict isn't capable of keeping agreements—hasn't the parent been disappointed on this score a number of times? If the parent wasn't able to cope with what the addict was up to before the so-called move, the parent won't be able to cope any better now. Bedlam is the order of the day, with the parent/addict struggle more intense than ever.

How to safeguard yourself from yourself

Once the addict is out of the house, the enemy—drug-addicted and alcoholic behavior—is gone also. But a powerful enemy remains behind: your mind. Nothing will trip you up faster than the lethal combination of your brain and your imagination. By comparison, it's easier to sever relations with your addict than with your own self-sabotaging capabilities. The brain is extremely vocal and will undermine you at every turn—making you doubt your decision to oust the addict, painting vivid pictures of the addict sitting confused and helpless in a strange place, showing you as having been impatient, unjust, and highly irrational.

By the time the brain is finished with you, you're ready to throw in the towel. Decisions you made that seemed so right at the time will now seem all wrong. But there are ways to preserve your decision as well as the peace you seek. Here they are.

Do nothing. Make a decision not to do anything else regarding the addict for at least one month.

Suppress nothing. Give your brain the podium. Listen carefully to everything it has to say. Let it rant and rave, even hurl accusations at you, so that its views are completely aired. Stay centered as you go through the process of answering each of the criticisms aimed at you. By calmly giving yourself the reasons for removing the addict, you'll see that you had no other choice—not if you and your brain wanted to survive, that is.

Ease your brain. If your brain won't relent, go over the same list of criticisms with a therapist (one who has dealt with drug and alcohol abuse) or with someone from a support group such as Al-Anon, Nar-Anon, Parents Anonymous, or Tough Love.

Steer clear. Don't, under any circumstances, get involved in conversations with people who have little or no experience in dealing with drug or alcohol addiction. Even the kindest, most compassionate friend may have trouble understanding your actions (much more on this in the next chapter).

Keep busy. Dedicate yourself to an all-absorbing project. Make a commitment to yourself that you'll finish this project. Let nothing, especially your brain, stand in your way.

Make a comeback. Renew relationships with family members (especially your spouse and other kids) and with friends who may have been shunted aside while the addict took center stage.

Don't isolate. A brain with a ton of negativity to dump somewhere likes nothing better than a captive audience: you.

You didn't leave the addict, the addict left you

There is one major realization that parents of children on drugs have to accept: The child is gone. His or her body may be present, but while under the influence of drugs or alcohol, the child is completely cut off from others. Drugs and alcohol act in such a way as to replace the person you've loved, raised, and cared for with a demented stranger. Parents tend to react to this intruder in the same way they would to a burglar breaking into their homes. The fact is, the chemically-addicted child *is* a burglar who has broken into your home and robbed you of your peace of mind.

This isn't science fiction. This is real. Except

that it seems unreal. Parents can't make out a report to missing children's organizations or have the police search the neighborhood for their children. Instead, they may continue on the futile path of trying to reach their chemically-addicted kids. That is, until they learn that there's nothing left to reach.

Remember them the way they were

Addicts, by the very nature of their disease, cast a pall over everything around them. They work with gloom and despair the way a potter works with clay, molding them into monuments too large for parents to blot out. The parent who can recall even a minimal pleasantry while in the midst of the addict is indeed lucky. Far more common is the addict's utter and complete disregard for harmony and brightness within the family experience or the preservation of cherished memories.

By permeating the atmosphere with negative energy, the addict manages to cheat the parent out of what would ordinarily have been moments to remember: the Thanksgiving meal, the high school graduation that never was, the close and loving bonding between parent and child. When the addict is finally gone, moved to another location, there may be very little to look back on that is beautiful and meaningful.

Fortunately, the addict cannot remove from the parent's box of memories how he or she was as a young child. That child is, somehow, still alive in a parent's heart. And certainly in a parent's photograph album. I often look at the pictures of my kids when young and remember the occasions that took place. There's a photo of my youngest son when he was just beginning to walk and talk. He stands teetering at the waterline on a beach. I remember asking him if he was going in the water and he, having deliberated for a moment, finally answered that no, he wasn't going in because it was "too wet." Then there's the photo of his brother slumped in the back of our station wagon after a trip to a beautiful castle in England where we were living at the time. Looking up at me, his tired words were: "I don't want to see one more beautiful thing."

The present may be marred by the ugliness of addiction, but the past is still pristine. All the fun times you had, the hopeful times, still exist.

In a society that asks us to kill off the past, this is the one time to preserve.

Hope: You're still entitled to it

Some addicts get into recovery. Other addicts don't. There's nothing to say that your addict won't eventually get tired of throwing his or her life away.

The main thing to remember is that regardless of what your addict decides to do, you mustn't throw *your* life away.

7

Other People Will Condemn You: Let Them

CAROLINE AND WILL'S STORY. Being publicly denounced by friends and family isn't an especially comfortable position to be in, as Caroline and Will have discovered. After having threatened to put their drug-addicted son—a youth of sixteen— out on the street unless he got into a recovery program, Caroline and Will became the focus of an unpleasant family onslaught which hasn't even begun to abate.

We sit in their home discussing how isolated they feel in their small midwestern hometown.

Their son, Jeremy, has made it clear to everyone with ears that he feels mistreated by his parents. He denies all allegations that he is a drug user or ever has been one. Predictably, Caroline and Will have not gone any further in trying to dissuade any of their inflamed family members from believing Jeremy's hang-dog story of parental abuse.

"What's the sense?" Caroline asks. "And anyway, who'd believe us? Jeremy is such an accomplished actor, he can make people believe anything he wants them to. Weren't Will and I fooled for the longest time? Besides all that, even if they did know, they'd never blame Jeremy. They'd blame us. They'd say his drug-taking was all our fault and if we'd been good parents to him in the first place he wouldn't have turned to drugs. That's the kind of thinking that comes from our family."

"In our family, you just push the dirt under the rug or it'll get pushed right into your face," Will says.

"Our big mistake was telling my mom," Caroline points out. "We told her all the details about Jeremy and his drug habit and you know what she asked? She asked us if we were sure that it wasn't *us* on drugs. The fact is, she didn't believe us. Then when we showed her some of Jeremy's drug paraphernalia, she went right into denial and that was that. Later, when we told her that we'd given Jeremy an ultimatum to either get off drugs or get out, all hell broke loose. She accused Will and me of slandering Jeremy and actually lying about his drug-taking just to get rid of him. I told her that if she didn't believe me all she needed to do was have Jeremy take a urine analysis, and she slammed the receiver down on me. Next thing we knew, she took Jeremy into her own home to live—without even informing us that she was doing this. She just marched into our house one day, picked him up, had him pack his things, and off they went—wouldn't say a word to us, although we know she's had plenty to say to others. She and the rest of the family have been totally hoodwinked by Jeremy, that's for sure."

"This thing has destroyed the relationships we had with both our families," Will says. "My own sister has called me every name in the book and refuses to have anything to do with us. Friends with kids in the same age group as Jeremy have completely abandoned us—and these were friends we'd had for years!"

"Do you feel you were doing the right thing coming up with the ultimatum?" I ask.

"Have you ever tried living with a junkie?" Caroline replies. "That kid almost drove us crazy with his lies and deception. We didn't know what was going on at first, but then we found Jeremy's bong. Turns out Jeremy was into all kinds of drugs including LSD. I was shocked beyond belief. I mean, I'd heard about this kind of thing, but I never expected to have it happen in my own home with my own son. We didn't know how he could afford drugs, but then everything fell into place: the missing cash from my purse, the missing household items, the money he was able to sneak from our credit cards, the beautiful diamond watch I thought I'd lost but hadn't really lost at all . . ."

"I hit the roof when I found out about all this drug business," Will says. "But Jeremy caught us completely off guard with his willingness to talk about it. He seemed very honest and straightforward. He told us he hated deceiving us. He said he loved us and didn't want to hurt us any more. He promised to go into a recovery program. We believed him when he said that he really wanted to stop taking drugs and needed our help. Of course we said we'd do anything we could, get him into a rehab, help him kick the habit. We told him that we were there for him one-hundred percent. But it didn't take long for us to realize that he was just stalling for time, trying to appease us. It was all a pack of lies. The only thing he wanted to do was use us."

"Suck our blood," Caroline puts in.

"Things came to a head when Jeremy continued taking drugs and refused to keep his promise about going into the rehab we'd found and arranged for him," Caroline continues. "He just point blank refused to go. Which is when we told him that he could either go into the rehab and count on us for support or he could stay on drugs and find another place to live. I guess that's when he put in an appeal to my mother. The amazing thing is that Jeremy is able to continue in high school, even gets good grades. To look at him, you'd think he was just another average, clean-cut American teenager. And that's just what he wants people to think. It's a great cover-up for him. Meanwhile, I'm afraid to go out of the house. The other day in the supermarket, a woman I never saw before walked right up to me and told me I was a monster."

"I've had a few business setbacks," Will says. "One of my clients whose son goes to the same school as Jeremy even put me down about the way we've handled things. Told me we should get down on our knees and beg for Jeremy's forgiveness. Do you believe this?"

Having been through a similar situation myself, yes, I do believe this.

The Art of the addict

Some of the best con men and women in the world are drug addicts and alcoholics. They have to be good—maintaining their chemical dependency depends upon it. To continue doing what they're doing—shooting up, sniffing in, and/or taking orally a variety of mind-altering chemicals—they must enlist the aid of others. This is mainly for the money to buy substances but also for those basic necessities (though of far less importance to them) such as shelter and the occasional meal.

The success of an addict's presentation and sales pitch is crucial to the success of his con. Confessing that he's an addict is risky although there is a trend to just "tell it as it is" about one's addictions and make it clear that the money asked for will, yes, go for substances. This trend, although it works sometimes, isn't as successful as other methods of soliciting funds. For the most part, telling the truth spells doom from the very start because most people regard addicts as sick, dishonest, irresponsible, criminally-minded beings. To counteract this general belief, many addicts strive to give a completely different impression, one that's intended to bring tears to the listener's eyes—the tirade of society's poor, innocent, misunderstood, unloved children who've been "thrown away" by their families.

They must convince would-be benefactors that their parents never cared about them, never praised them, found them to "be in the way," and finally got rid of them. These accounts rarely differ from one addict to another. (Why change a story that works?) All that matters to them is that they succeed in moving the benefactor to a place of righteous anger against the parents and at the same time, sympathy and pity for themselves.

When one of my children was in a rehabilitation center several years ago recovering from a serious addiction, I was informed during an orientation session that, along with the other parents and loved ones visiting their addicts in recovery, I would be required to attend weekly Al-Anon meetings held on the grounds. The reason given was that it wasn't only the addict who was sick and in need of help but, in most cases, the family as well, something I could agree with. These meetings were set up so that we could, first of all, explore the intricate workings of an addict's brain. And, equally importantly, we would explore why so many of us parents, wives, husbands, brothers and sisters are willing to accept the role of caretaker and rescuer.

During the first of these meetings, the director of the center, a recovered drug user himself, glanced out at us—the parents, spouses, and siblings of the addicts—sitting before him in a small theater. Then, with a wry grin, he commented on how easy it would be for him to "work the room" or, in other words, get from any and all of us whatever he wanted, even though we were total strangers. All he'd have to do, he told us, was to give us the same old spiel he had given hundreds of other people during his drug days. With a practiced sincerity and with his "sell" down pat, it wouldn't take him long, he said, to persuade us to take him into our homes, into our hearts, give him money, or even co-sign for a car loan. Or all of the above.

Sounds impossible, but judging from what I've seen and heard (and done) myself, there is definitely truth in what the director was saying. There is no one more genuine-seeming or more persuasive than an addict. And there is no one more gullible than the people who are willing to lend that addict an ear.

The director indicated that in referring to drug addicts and alcoholics, he wasn't referring to those on the street who are obvious panhandlers. Rather he meant the addicts who look and act in a seemingly normal, rational manner and who, just incidentally, happen to have their well-rehearsed hard-luck story ready to recite.

By slipping into the abject, forlorn persona of a victim, an addict will relate how his mother and father, for no reason at all—at least for no reason *he* could possibly discern—threw him out of the house, and said that they wanted nothing further to do with him. Statements like this are intended to carry a certain shock value regarding the callousness with which the addict's parents have so easily discarded him. They're also intended to tug at the heartstrings (and purse strings) of the listener, thereby creating massive amounts of sympathy. The addict knows he has struck gold when the new ally vows to help, in any way possible, this poor kid so vulnerable to the world, this *orphan.*

Where has the addict learned the art of persuasion so well? He's had plenty of practice.

Parents are the people upon whom addicts first hone their incredible skills of verbal persuasion. It's a gift that lasts as long as a parent's patience and naivete last—which can be, and sometimes is, decades. And when that source has dried up, with the parent finally declining to bow to the addict's persuasive powers any longer, the addict needs only to go off and find another willing party. *Any* willing party will do. Security for the addict means always having a rescuer at hand. It doesn't matter who that rescuer is as long as he or she can supply what is needed.

Addicts seem to be equipped with an uncanny talent for finding the soft spot in a person's heart. With an approach that's hard to resist, an addict can usually string together a series of benefactors. The people most susceptible to the addict's persuasive art are apt to be (after parents) other relatives and family friends. The bigger the family, the better. Addicts will get to *everybody* in due course. The target can be a distant relative who has never even *seen* the addict, but is nevertheless a blood relation. Being of the same blood is an extraordinary link and a very serviceable calling card. Hardly ever is the addict turned away point blank. Often, it only takes one phone call from the addict explaining his or her dilemma with "cruel, unfeeling parents," for the now-outraged distant relative to lend this "child victim" immediate financial support and to bombard the parents with phone calls and letters demanding that they do the same.

In many cases, these well-meaning but misguided people fail to investigate anything further than what the addict has told them. From my experience, they almost never ask the parents' side of the story. Mostly, they just leap into the picture assuming the role of rescuer. Their interference in situations that don't concern them winds up doing far more harm than good.

So convincing is the addict that any defense on the parents' part is often seen as suspicious, especially when the parent is feeling outraged by the intrusion. Emotional outbursts by the parents merely confirm to the "rescuer" what the addict has already indicated, that the parent has an unbridled temper, is unstable, and obviously wants to unload the kids on the side of the road.

What further proof do they need?

Crazier than the addict

The parent of an addict very often appears truly certifiable. By comparison, the addict appears totally sane.

This is because parents often succumb to the stress and worry they feel over their addicted children. Both physical and mental ailments assail them. They can't sleep at night. They either lose a lot of weight or gain a lot of weight—never stay stable. They will take anything another person may say about them as malicious and will react strongly at what they perceive to be a personal slight. If these parents of addicts have managed to stay married to one another, they will frequently engage in horrendous blaming sessions. They will cry easily, sometimes in public places. They will rant and rave at co-workers, store clerks, friends, relatives, and, much of the time, each other.

While addicts are obsessed with their drugs, badly affected parents are obsessed with the addict. They can talk of nothing else. After a while, with their endless litanies regarding the addict, they chase away practically every loyal friend or supporter they ever had. Another sign of their obsessive traits is the fear of leaving the house. And if being called out of the house bothers them, being called out of town will almost certainly create a panic attack. Parents of addicts feel that they have to be right beside the phone just in case the addict calls.

For the most part, these parents do little or nothing to lower their high anxiety levels. They don't know how to relax or enjoy the things that are good about their lives. Nor are they usually engaged in any of the available stress reduction options such as yoga, meditation, exercise, and therapeutic guidance to help ease the vast emotional strain they're under.

Some parents of addicts capitulate to drugs (prescription and otherwise) and alcohol themselves. Talk of committing suicide is common. The actual act is also common.

If people think these parents are unhinged it's because, in a very real sense, they are.

Who cares what people say? Maybe you do

Dealing with an addict is one thing, but when the

addict has enlisted the aid of what now appears to be a growing army of supporters—most of it originating from one's own family or group of friends—parents get even more bent out of shape. Through the vast networking system that operates within *every* family, parents who've removed the addicts from their homes find themselves suddenly in the wrong with everybody. Telephone calls abound. These are usually from people who've never in their lives had to deal with an addict but are willing to believe every word of "young Jason's" or "young Emily's" harrowing tale of mistreatment. These people are more than willing to volunteer their opinions on how you should have handled the situation, plus what you can do now to make up for your dreadful bungling of the job.

Of course, the more convincing the addict's version, the less convincing the parent's. This is a classic situation found in thousands of families today. Addicts latch onto their victim roles with Academy award-winning performances, taking every precaution not to let other family members witness the bizarre effects upon them from the chemicals they're taking.

And even if found out, the addicts can (and do) blame the parents for all of their misfortunes. Those who are sympathetic to the woes of the addict—and uneducated in the way of addiction—are apt to heap even more blame upon the parents. This, in addition to the blame parents may be already dumping upon themselves, makes for a gargantuan burden.

The parent as people-pleaser

Things can really get bad if the parent is someone who has always needed the approval of others. For such a parent, confrontation with family members or friends or co-workers (or anybody else, for that matter) is excruciating. Caring what others think leads to feelings of insecurity, guilt, fear, inadequacy, and self-recrimination. Feeling that they must accommodate the world, most people-pleasing parents allow themselves to be talked into just about anything. Making unwise decisions becomes almost inevitable.

Sometimes, besieged people-pleasing parents, who originally felt they were making the right decision by ousting the addict, now come to believe that they are at fault. This is when, severely brow-beaten and weakened by relatives and friends, they allow the addict, without restrictions or conditions of any kind, back into the house.

Here are some steps to help people-pleasing parents achieve a more balanced outlook:

Accept where other people are. Keep in mind that just by *having* an addicted child, you automatically qualify as a bad parent in the eyes of many—a prime target on the gossiper's hit list.

Forget where other people are. Ignore what other people think, say, or do. They have no power over you. The only person who has power over you is yourself.

Do some research. Look into your past for the reasons you became a people-pleaser in the first place. No doubt you did it in order to be liked. But honestly, besides having avoided getting yourself seriously *disliked*, have there ever been any real benefits? Haven't you always felt slightly foolish in the role of people-pleaser?

Count your losses. Think of all you've lost by neglecting yourself. While multitudes of others have gained by your sacrifices, you've been stuck in the same old role year after year. You give, you serve, you lose.

Put your people-pleaser on strike. Try to understand how unnatural being a people-pleaser is. Look, everybody acts like a jerk sometimes, shouts sometimes, says stupid things sometimes, is selfish sometimes. That's just being a normal person. People-pleasers seem to think they have to act with decorum at all times, suppressing all the human emotions just to look good. In the end, being a people-pleaser is tantamount to being just plain dishonest.

Take responsibility. Come to understand how being a people-pleaser may have seriously contributed to the situation you're now in. By pleasing everybody —especially the addict—you have, in effect, cheated them of their opportunities to learn and grow from their own life experiences. In the end, being a people-pleaser has severely selfish overtones.

How to cope with a meddling relative or friend

As the average meddler will tell you: "I don't care what your child has done. I don't care if he's come after you with an ax. I don't care if he's tried to burn the house down with you in it. I don't care if he's robbed you blind. Parents do not throw their children, drug-addicted, alcoholic, or otherwise, out of the house. They take their child in their arms and tell him or her that everything is going to be all right, that you'll work out the problems together."

Yeah, right.

It is amazing the number of people—some of them mental-health professionals—who will advise parents that the way to deal with an addict is to assure him or her that together the two of you will deal with the situation.

It's not as if you haven't already gone that same stale route a million times.

The thing is, are you, as the parent of an out-and-out, violent, drug-crazed addict, going to try this one more time? Or are you going to take some positive action that will drown out the voice of the meddler?

Here are a few things to remember.

1. You don't have to explain your actions to anyone, especially to people who are not directly involved in dealing with your addict. You may wish to explain once, and possibly even twice. But don't waste your time or your breath after that.

2. Give yourself some time to process your sense of rage, frustration, and hurt. It's perfectly normal to feel anger at being imposed upon by so many "experts" who start spewing advice without your invitation and without the remotest idea of the addict's destructive streak.

3. After you've calmed down, know that while being judged is unpleasant, unfair, and unavoidable, that's the way it is. There is nothing you can do except accept it as the price you have to pay in order to straighten out your life and reclaim your sanity.

4. Inform the various meddlers hounding you that you will call *them* if you need their help, that they shouldn't call *you*. You may want to screen all calls if the meddlers keep contacting you.

5. Expend no further energy on the meddler. You have far more important things to do than trying to win the meddler over or staying in a resentful frame of mind which is neither constructive nor healing.

6. Should the meddler intercede on the part of the addict by supplying some or all of the things you've withdrawn—such as food, shelter, and money (especially money), stay detached. It may only be a matter of time before the meddler discovers the devious and destructive nature of the addict for him or herself. On the other hand, it may turn out that the meddler never discovers these traits, even if they're staring him or her right in the face. Either way, you don't have to be involved.

7. Differentiate between what is your business and what is not your business. The main message here is that what other people think of you is *none* of your business.

You may never be accepted for your actions: That's okay

Once there has been a breach in the way people have treated you, there's usually no road back. And even if there were, would you want it?

Parents of addicts find that when they lose a child to drugs or alcohol, they lose a lot of other people also: namely, the people who felt it was their place to admonish them during their most stressful moments.

And while it's a sad situation, at least you know where you stand. The act of freeing yourself from the day-to-day struggles with an addict automatically brings refreshing change into your life. With that change you'll want to select the people you deal with on a completely different basis than before. Everybody deserves loving, supportive people around them.

And that includes you.

8

Supportive People: They're More Available Than You Think

TINA AND RAY'S STORY. It's a Saturday afternoon in East Los Angeles, a day off for many of the people in the neighborhood. But it's not a day off when it comes to the sound of firearms. Their loud reports are easily heard from Tina and Ray's small apartment.

"Another drive-by shooting," Ray explains. "We used to get this at night only. Now we get it in broad daylight."

"This is a war zone," Tina adds, "and you never know who's going to be killed next. Usually the drug dealers go around killing each other, but a lot of innocent people get in the way and are mowed down."

Tina and Ray have already lost one son to a violent death, shot execution-style in front of their apartment building. Unfortunately, their sorrows haven't stopped there. Two other sons are out there playing the same odds. According to Ray, not only are his boys drug-addicted, but they also deal drugs. Tina tells me that one of the boys is only fourteen.

"Our kids are out there with the drugs and the guns," she says. "And there's nothing we can do to stop them. We tried everything. We tried talking to them, trying to get them to stop. But they're wild. They don't listen to us."

"Our whole family is like this," Ray says. "Uncles, cousins, nephews. We don't know anybody who doesn't have something like this. We came from Mexico for a better life and this is what we got."

"When we lost Jimmy, we didn't know where to turn," Tina says. "We have the church and we have the group we meet with—a parents group. Without those two things, we'd be lost."

Tina and Ray rarely miss a Parents Anonymous meeting these days. By attending, they feel they're staying in touch with the sane world.

"The people in the group help us get through our bad times," Tina says. "And we help them get through theirs. There's so much tragedy! Last week, a woman told us how her son overdosed on a bad batch of heroin going around called 'Super Buick' and needed four people to restrain him. Then the kid's heart gave out and he died."

"Every week, there's some story like this. You

can't get away from it," Ray replies. "But we keep going back because it's the only place we can go where people understand."

Support groups: a parent's best friend

Like Tina and Ray, I also found that I could benefit by attending support groups. The powerful Twelve Step meetings, so called because of their twelve philosophical tenets, help addicts and non-addicts alike recover from the effects of substance abuse. My weekly routine included several Twelve Step meetings that I wouldn't have dreamed of missing. Even if I was away from home, I could always locate a meeting in any city, small town, or even remote area any time I wanted one—which was often. For a period of about five years, support group meetings were the mainstay of my life. Without them, I would most certainly have foundered.

The meetings I attended most were the Nar-Anon meetings. These are for family and friends of drug-addicted people. Nar-Anon supplied me with the tools I needed in dealing with the addicts in my life. Al-Anon, with more of an emphasis on alcohol-addicted individuals, was also very helpful. Additionally, I sometimes went to Parents Anonymous meetings to be in the sole company of parents like myself. And I went to Adult Children of Alcoholics because there was a history of alcoholism in my family which I'd keenly felt as a child growing up.

And, even though I wasn't chemically addicted myself, I went to the occasional Alcoholics Anonymous or Narcotics Anonymous meeting.

These latter meetings gave me an insight into the plight of people who have been struck with the disease of chemical dependence. I am always in awe by the courageous way many of them forged ahead in their quests for recovery. Their determination to live a chemical-free existence is an inspiration. The hard-won victories they've achieved aren't something to be dismissed easily. One of the worst aspects of the disease is the intense desire, on a minute-to-minute basis, to drink or drug again. Temptation is tantalizingly close at all times and yet recovering alcoholics and drug addicts—through sheer will power, and by putting their trust in a being higher than themselves—defy the odds again and again. As they say in all Twelve Step programs, "one day at a time."

About Nar-Anon and Al-Anon

It was in the company of other parents of drug addicts and alcoholics, as well as their children, spouses, siblings, and friends, that I found my strongest support. Nar-Anon became, very quickly, the center of my universe because of what it provided.

In this rarefied atmosphere of understanding, I was free to discuss openly any and all problems related to my role as the parent of chemically-addicted children. Surrounded by loving people, I knew I wouldn't be judged in the way parents of addicts are so often judged by family, friends, and society in general.

Safeguarded by a strict doctrine of confidentiality, people felt safe in sharing their deepest feelings. Most of their accounts were strikingly similar to my own. By hearing the stories of others, I was relieved to learn that we were all dealing with the same problems. The feeling of isolation I had been experiencing disappeared.

By joining various support groups, I picked up practical solutions on how to combat the many destructive hallmarks of the chemically-addicted child: the anger, the violence, the lies, the thievery, the destruction of private and public property, the bouts with the police, the days in court, the financial burden.

I also picked up practical solutions on dealing with my emotions regarding the addicts in my family: the worries concerning their whereabouts, their suicide threats, their refusals to get help, and the thoughts of them sharing needles in this day of AIDS. I learned to deal with my worries of them living on the streets. Of them perhaps selling their bodies on the streets. Of them dying in the streets. I learned to deal with the deep sorrow of seeing them wasting their lives away, not giving a damn about their futures, squandering whatever talents they may have had. Last, I learned to deal with the heart-gripping sense of loss I felt in the way that the disease had, in effect, stolen my children away from me along with any fulfilling years we might have had together.

Learning about codependence

A very important aspect of being in these support groups was the discovery that I had to take responsibility for my own actions. This was probably my biggest eye-opener. If I thought all the problems I was having were due solely to the addict, I was wrong. Through a series of revelations brought about by what I learned in Nar-Anon and Al-Anon, I soon saw that I was just as responsible, and in many ways just as sick, as the addicts in my life. It was in these meeting rooms that I first heard the term "codependent." It means someone who takes complete responsibility for another person while at the same time ignoring his or her own needs.

A popular Twelve Step joke goes like this:

Question: *What does a codependent see when committing suicide off the Golden Gate Bridge?*

Answer: *Somebody else's life passing before his eyes.*

Identifying myself as a codependent, I realized I wasn't living my life, but the lives of my children.

By placing myself in a subservient position, I had very little concern for my own well-being, fulfillment, or happiness.

Codependence, as I was to learn, is just as much a malady as is drug or alcohol addiction. There's as much risk to the codependent as there is to the addict in terms of life being cut short through disease or suicide.

Other benefits of Nar-Anon and Al-Anon

After I recognized how well I fit the role of a codependent, Nar-Anon and Al-Anon taught me necessary and valuable guidelines for how to take the focus off my addicted children with their problems and faults, and turn it where it belonged, on myself. This was done mainly through the act of letting go and the art of detachment.

Finally, there was the companionship and fellowship that I needed during those dark, lonely times. There was a long period when things were so unendingly bleak, when there appeared to be no hope on the horizon, and my meetings became my rock. On one particular gloomy Sunday which I remember well, I strung together a group of meetings that would last from early morning to late night. I drove from one meeting location to the other, needful of only one thing: to be with the only people on earth who truly understood the dreadful effects of chemical-dependency upon one's children and oneself.

About the Twelve Steps

The Twelve Steps of Nar-Anon, Al-Anon, Parents Anonymous, and Codependents Anonymous are a great aid to parents who have taken upon themselves not just caring for their alcoholic and drug-addicted children, but also the responsibility for those children's choices.

What the steps do, in essence, is to create a new, practical reality which allows parents of addicts to step back and view the past with clarity and the present and future with strength. They also help put aside traditional parenting notions which can never work when the child is an addict. Mainly, the Twelve Steps in this context present a picture that's much larger than the parent/child relationship.

The first step urges parents of addicts to admit to themselves that they are powerless over chemical substances, and that their lives have become unmanageable. Parents who've tried to curb a child's use of drugs and alcohol and have been defeated at every turn will know what that powerlessness is all about. They'll also see how their lives had gone to seed before accepting their powerlessness.

The second and third steps ask the parent to vacate the role of mighty arbiter and to turn the entire mess over to a higher power, perhaps a spiritual or religious inspiration or a source of nature.

Step four sometimes presents an obstacle,

because it requires parents to take a fearless moral inventory of themselves. For the first time in the steps, it now appears that parents may have some flaws in their personalities, flaws they'll have to address. Dealing with this isn't always easy.

The fifth step asks parents to actually *admit* these flaws to their higher powers of choice, to themselves, and to another person. Again, not always easy.

Parting with the flaws is the message of step six. This calls for asking one's higher power to remove all one's defects of character.

Step seven goes on to ask for the removal of all shortcomings. This step centers primarily around balancing the ego.

The eighth step calls for the conjuring up of memories: Parents are asked to make a list of all persons they have harmed and to make amends to each and every one.

Step nine urges parents to make these amends directly to the person affected (sometimes considered a difficult task), except when doing so would injure them or others.

Step ten helps keep parents from slipping back into old ways by reminding them to continue taking personal inventory and by admitting times when they are wrong.

Seeking to keep parents in conscious contact with their higher power is the aim of step eleven. It also asks for the knowledge and ability to carry out that which one's higher power requests.

The final step asks for parents to share with others the principles of all the Twelve Steps so that knowledge of the benefits can become widespread.

With all the turning over and letting go that's so much a part of Twelve Step programs, parents of addicts begin to feel a peace they haven't experienced for years. The Twelve Steps work gently and patiently on a parent's consciousness. They offer substantial rewards to anyone willing to get in and clean house, so to speak. This calls for an honest evaluation of oneself, exposing warts and all.

Tough Love: giving you the courage to do what's necessary

Tough Love is not one of the Twelve Step programs. But what it offers is just as valuable. Many parents arrive on its doorstep feeling dazed and victimized by their addicted children. These parents are exhausted, beaten down, and unable to get a foothold on solid ground. Usually they are at the end of their tethers, having long endured the destructive actions of addicted children who are well past the rehabilitation stage. Heartbreaking as it is, there are such children—the unreachable ones who cannot and will not abide a life free of chemical dependency.

The main function of Tough Love is to help parents free themselves from the stranglehold these children have on them. Participants in the Tough Love process are parents who've been in exactly the same position as the new arrivals. They, too, were once in the same desperate straits, not knowing where to turn or what to do. Very few of them have ever seen signs of recovery in their children, but they exhibit marked proof of recovery in themselves.

Newcomers are welcomed by these more experienced parents. Their stories are heard. Their requests are heard. In Tough Love, as in the Twelve Step meetings, help is never given unless it's asked for. But once it is asked for, it is given freely and compassionately. That help consists of guiding newcomers through the truly horrible exercise in removing the addict from the home.

Plans are made, dates are set, and alternate housing for the addict is arranged. Informing the addict of the impending change can be tricky, as there is often a violent reaction. This is where some (or as many as necessary) of the other parents step in to help and lend support. Addicts tend to become pacified in the face of a crowd and often cooperate.

Tough Love then helps parents maintain their newly liberated status. Addicts will campaign in any number of ways to be allowed back into the home. They'll use manipulation, threats, accusations, and guilt tactics. Some parents can withstand this barrage, others succumb. Tough Love helps them to build resistance and secure their position.

As parents eventually learn, trying to get an addict into recovery is futile. It is only when the addict is good and ready that he or she will take action. If ever. The same is true for parents of addicts. No one can tell them they shouldn't live in a toxic atmosphere. When they're ready to make the change, they will. Tough Love is there to help in what can be a very difficult time of transition.

The ultimate goal: learning to support yourself

By joining a support group, the wheels of progress go into motion immediately toward changing destructive patterns in the parent/addict relationship. But a support group isn't forever. Or it shouldn't be. The main aim of support groups is to help train parents to support themselves mentally and emotionally. This isn't something that happens overnight. Some parents have to sit in support groups for years before bringing about any major changes in their lives, while other parents take charge right away.

If a support group can give parents of addicts the tools they need to a) separate their priorities from the addict's, b) allow for the addict to make his or her own mistakes without interfering, and c) feel good about themselves, then the support group has done its job.

How to join a parents support group

Listings for Nar-Anon and Al-Anon don't always

appear in your phone book, but you can usually find a listing for Alcoholics Anonymous.

By calling your nearest AA headquarters, you can obtain a list of local Twelve Step meetings which can include those of Nar-Anon, Al-Anon, and Parents Anonymous. (If you live in a rural area, you can call the AA headquarters in the nearest city.) Narcotics Anonymous and Alcoholics Anonymous meetings welcome non-addicts and non-alcoholics to their meetings. Please check your local listings as to which meetings are "open" to the public.

Another helpful source of information will be your local newspaper. The name of the specific meeting—along with dates, times, and locations—is normally listed in the events pages.

The telephone book, directory information, or your local newspaper are your best bets in locating Tough Love meetings.

When you've become acquainted with support group meetings, you'll be surprised as to how many are held daily in your vicinity.

9

Healing: Start with Yourself

BETTY'S STORY. A well-known author[1] and lecturer on meditation and dreamwork, Betty Bethards is also a counselor. Once in a while, her client will be a drug addict at the end of his rope; most often, it's a parent or a set of parents at the end of theirs.

Her last counseling session for the day is over and Betty comes out of her office with a smile. She's a vivacious woman whose grounded energy you feel right away.

On a foggy San Francisco night seven years ago, Betty's son, a young man of twenty-one, met his death when his motorcycle skidded into an abutment at the entrance of the Golden Gate Bridge. His blood alcohol level had been 1.1.

As a counselor, Betty has helped many clients

deal with tragedies stemming from their children's drug and alcohol use. Working with these parents, her emphasis has always been on self-healing. With the death of her own son, she had to utilize the tools she had created for her clients.

"Chris was an alcoholic," Betty says. "I knew that he was going to die. It was just a matter of time. He'd had many near-misses as the result of his drinking, including one the year before when he'd broken every bone in his face along with his collar-bone and several ribs in a car accident. That didn't stop him from drinking: He was right back at it soon as he was out of the hospital.

"Eventually, when the police came to the door after the accident, they didn't have to say anything. In fact, I told them that I knew why they were there. I was just grateful that he hadn't killed anyone else on the road. So you can say I was prepared for the worst. But that didn't mean I didn't have to do a lot of healing regardless. Those first months were rough. His death took everything out of me. I just talked to myself the way I would talk to someone coming to see me and I learned, first-hand, that I could be my own healer, my own best friend."

There's a calm about Betty that has as much to do with being practical and mature as it does with being an inspiration to others. I ask what she considers to be the most essential form of healing.

"Nurturing yourself," she answers. "Many parents

of alcoholics or drug addicts run the gamut from mild self-dislike to severe self-hatred. That's because they blame themselves for their kid's addictions. If they simply understood that there is such a thing as free will, that everyone has choices, they could understand that they had far less to do with how their children have turned out than they think. So the first thing to recognize is that they couldn't have done anything to prevent their children from becoming addicted to drugs or alcohol and that all they can do now is to take care of themselves as best they can. This means to drop the "poor me" victim act and to start appreciating themselves, start nurturing themselves. Mainly, they need to start seeing themselves as the beautiful, worthwhile people they are.

"The big stumbling block is that a lot of parents don't know how to break away from the old ways and get into the new," Betty says. "The first thing they have to do is to let go. Accept things as they are. This helps us keep a better perspective. The willingness to release the drug-addicted child also works to release ourselves. And to start building our own lives again. The faster a parent gets into this constructive way of thinking, the faster the progress. I have some parents who've dragged themselves in here looking like they were dead and have since done a wonderful job of restructuring their lives. It was hard for them as it is for all of us to let go, but there's no healing without this step.

"The healing part was the fun part for me," Betty laughs. "I'm a born hedonist. I like having fun, going for walks on the beach or in the redwoods, being with high-energy people. But more than anything else, I enjoy the inner journey, going deep within spiritually to learn about myself. I really feel that the only reason we're here on earth is to know ourselves. There's enough to do in that one area to last a lifetime. And most of what we learn is fascinating. I'm lucky because I know there's only one person I can change and that's me. I'm constantly striving to be the best me I can be.

"There are a lot of tools to work with and they're available to everyone if they'll just open themselves to the vast possibilities," Betty affirms. "It only takes a little venturing out from a person's shell to discover a whole new world. The main thing is for people to keep their energy high. When it's high, things don't bother you as much. You can be in a room full of alcoholics or drug addicts and you find that you can detach from them all. Suddenly, the guilt trips and manipulations they're pulling on you don't work anymore. And boy, are they surprised! If you used to be a pushover, you no longer are. Addicts go crazy over that because it means you're no longer giving them your power."

Through going to Betty's lectures over the years I have learned many tools of survival which I've incorporated in this chapter. But the subject of energy is, as Betty says, the most important in terms of healing oneself.

Energy. I had none. I was so stuck in my kids' problems with drugs, I took everything they dished out and it always hit me in one particular spot. Right in the solar plexus, the area in the human body where anxiety resides. I had no self-protection, no idea of self-preservation. It was a wonder that I could operate at all or earn a living. My performance was at its lowest as was my interest in work, hobbies, the world scene, and sex.

Betty talked of nurturing oneself. I was as far away from that possibility as anyone could be. I was so unaware of my own needs that I never even thought about nurturing or taking care of myself. So imbued with guilt and remorse was I that anything pleasant that occurred in my life met with an unqualified "I didn't deserve that" notation in my brain.

Funny, I never used the "I don't deserve that" approach with my own kids when they became addicted. Their abuse was commonplace, the expected thing.

Turning all this around and nurturing myself was probably the hardest task I ever had. Following along the lines that Betty described, I first had to let go. Let go of the kids, their problems, their choices, their destructive natures, their violence. Parents don't do this in a half hour. It takes work and commitment. And a desire to see the sun shine again.

I found that if I was able to stay true to myself and speak my truth whenever my drug-addicted kids were trying to take my power away, I was doing great.

Following are some healing techniques I learned from Betty and some I've devised for myself. These measures put me on the road to true healing. The same can happen for you.

Self-love: a great place to start

Self-Love? Ugh! Some parents reading this may think this is weird. But what they don't know is that healing won't work unless they make a concerted effort to well, yes, love themselves. It's as simple as that.

First, parents have to identity what self-love is. Basically, it's the same thing as loving someone else. By offering themselves the warmth, caring, and respect that they would normally offer someone else, they're starting to get the picture.

But how many parents do this? How many parents have *ever* done this? From the time we are small, we are taught in our homes, schools, and churches to love other people and to treat ourselves as selfless martyrs. We go through life loving others, giving to others, doing for others, rejoicing for others. But what about ourselves? We tend to serve ourselves life's leftovers.

We've been trained to look at praise, affection, and approval as something coming exclusively from outside of ourselves, from another human being or an achievement. To have a capacity for self-love there has to be, as an inner resource, a strong link with ourselves that we can draw on whenever we need it. This is the element parents of addicts have denied themselves. They hardly ever see themselves as individuals who need to give to themselves. Rather, all gifts are outgoing, rarely appreciated by the addicts receiving them. If anything, addicts generally regard gift-bearing parents with contempt. The very simple and plain fact is: If a parent can't genuinely love him or herself, how can anyone else?

Parents who know that true healing starts with self-love aren't concerned with public opinion. The mere act of letting go of one's addicted child can be perceived by others as selfish and uncaring. Parents who love themselves are able to detach from such opinion and get on with their lives.

Additionally, they know they can re-invent themselves. In a continual life-long inventory, parents who love themselves will learn to throw out the things they don't like about themselves and keep the things they do.

Parents who love themselves allow others, including their addicted children, to walk their own walk. They can be happy for their children's successes and sad for their failures; but they always maintain the overall view that each of us is on a special path, our destinations revealed only to ourselves as we journey on. They know that they don't have to deal with or see their children when those children are in an addicted or abusive state. Once parents have done everything possible to sway an addicted child off substances, their duty toward that child is over. They don't have to be part of the manipulation or the violence perpetrated by the addict. They can even give themselves permission to get out of the relationship altogether.

Lastly, they know they have the right to be happy and enjoy their lives. They can put their efforts into creating an environment around them that's perfect for them. They never have to apologize to anyone, including themselves, for being happy.

Meditation: your own energy generator

Meditation isn't new. It has been practiced since ancient times. In more recent years, however, it had become associated less as a health-giving resource and more as an laughable pastime of hippies, psychics, and eccentrics.

Now the A.M.A. describes meditation as a physically calming therapy for body and mind, a valuable therapy for reducing stress levels and to help treat stress-related disorders.[2] Some doctors prescribe it for people who are ill, people who have been ill recently, and people who don't want to become ill.

What exactly happens when a person meditates? The body is a series of electromagnetic impulses. It responds to meditation the way a weak battery reacts to jumper cables. Meditation recharges the body, sending electrical currents to each and every part of it. The benefits are many. Energy surges through the blood vessels to the brain so that the body feels renewed, refreshed. The effect is stunning because when a person feels good such maladies as fear, anger, resentment, and depression become less potent and frequently disappear altogether. Parents of addicts benefit greatly when they meditate, because they're less prone to react to the manipulations, tantrums, and violence of their addicts.

For Betty Bethards' method of meditation, you sit quietly in a chair with a straight spine so that the energy has a clear channel to flow upward. You sit with palms together for ten minutes and then palms upward on the lap for ten minutes, as energy is generated in the body. An important step to remember is to close down at the end of twenty minutes in order to protect the energy you've built up. Closing down is achieved by closing both hands into fists on your lap while envisioning yourself in a balloon of white light that extends a mile around you. This creates your own personal protective shield that guards you from picking up the negative energy of other people.

By practicing this exercise daily for twenty minutes, parents of addicts begin to feel its relaxing and health-giving benefits almost immediately. The addict may act up just as much as ever but, by meditating, the parent can detach more easily; no longer is every crisis with the addict regarded as the end of the world.

This meditation is a twenty-minute-a-day investment. But it enables the parent of an addict to survive the other twenty-three hours and forty minutes.

Develop a sense of humor: You're going to need one

Drug addiction or alcoholism in one's child is nothing to laugh about. But some of the situations around addiction are. Especially those that have to do with your own reactions to the addict.

How many times have you gone on wild goose chases in behalf of the addict? Or been tricked into doing something you definitely did not want to do? Just thinking back on what a fool you'd allowed yourself to become should be worth a few laughs! To dispel the pull of negativity so frequently related to substance abuse, there's nothing like lightening up, seeing the ludicrous situation for what it really is.

Substance abusers hate laughter. They prefer to remain in a dark, midnight world where everyone is in mourning. That's fine, but you don't have to remain there with them. In fact, the sooner you put on a cheerful face, the sooner you'll heal. Things won't seem as hopeless if you can infuse some light into the matter.

Maintain your boundaries, retain your energy

When parents dwell on the misfortune of the addicted child or argue with that child, they automatically deplete whatever resources of energy they may possess. Even that new supply of energy they received by meditating disappears. They are, in essence, diminishing their power and their well-being, dropping them to zero.

The major benefit of setting strong boundaries with an addicted child is the preservation of one's own life force. Those boundaries must be kept even when the addict isn't in the picture. That's because energy will rise and fall depending upon the parent's thought patterns. If there's nothing but a clutter of depressing thoughts and visions accompanied by fear and regret, the parent will be drained. But by continually affirming positive thoughts and images, a parent can raise his or her energy level and keep it high. Therefore, parents must create strong boundaries with themselves as well as their addicted children. By not allowing either themselves or their addicts to trespass over them, parents are essentially safeguarding what is rightfully theirs.

Energy is like money. If you give it all away, you'll have nothing left for yourself.

Tune in to your dreams

The value of analyzing dreams is usually underestimated. When a troubled parent has no remedies for the disasters in his or her life, dreams often supply the answer. By charting dreams on a daily basis, parents can actually begin to see the negative patterns they've set up, the blocks that keep them stuck in all the petty little dramas with the addict. For example, a dream in which the parent is in a sinking boat says the obvious: that the parent is drowning in a sea of emotions. Another common dream has the addicted child driving a car with the parent as the passenger. The child is wildly reckless and the parent is powerless. The message of this dream is that addicted children can become all-powerful (in the driver's seat) if the parent allows it, placing the parent in true jeopardy.

Many parents claim that they do not dream. It's not true. Everybody dreams. But when you have little or no energy, it can be difficult to retrieve the message of your dreams. When you start working on your energy, increasing it steadily in time, the ability to remember dreams follows. Still, dream analysis is a dedicated discipline which calls for parents to make a concerted effort to recall what they dream at night. By placing a pen and pad of paper on their nightstand tables (to write down the dream immediately upon awakening) and affirming that they will have a dream and remember it, parents stimulate their subconscious desire for dream recall.

Visualizations: getting away from it all without even leaving the room

As said earlier, your energy rises and ebbs according to your thoughts. If you stay in the negative, your energy will be nil. If you concentrate on happier thoughts, your energy will rise to the occasion. Try it. Think of a bad time and try to locate your energy level. If you can't find it, it's probably because your energy is altogether depleted! Now think of a time when life was great: Suddenly you feel a surge of positive energy (and if you don't feel it right away, don't worry, it's there).

One way to elevate your energy is to think positive thoughts all the time, a near-impossible human feat. But you cultivate a more beneficial energy flow if you can see yourself in bright, healing light.

Visualization is an excellent and easy way to achieve this. By spending a few minutes mentally each day in the setting of your choice—it can be in a garden or on a cloud or on a beautiful beach or any scene in your mind that you prefer—you will soon come to see that this is your way of getting away from it all. And you don't even have to pack a suitcase.

Affirmations: be careful what you ask for

What do you want? Listen to your heart and then make your request. That is an affirmation. When you continually ask for what you want, there is a cumulative effect. It's like constantly wishing good things upon yourself.

Parents of addicts need to counterbalance all the negativity they are experiencing by affirming, in a concentrated manner, some of the rich rewards available to everybody.

How do you best affirm what you want? Perhaps you say or think each thing at the end of your meditation session. Or, perhaps you write it out each day in a *mandala* (visual, graphic) form. By simply drawing a circle and placing a star in the middle of it, you've made your own *mandala*. Now it's time to fill that circle with all the goals you wish to realize.

Some goals you may choose to affirm in your *mandala* are the following:

1. The quest for *peace*. As the parent of an addict, you probably haven't felt the soothing, silent glow of peace around you in a long time. But it can be regained. "Inner peace is coming to me easily and effortlessly."

2. The *wisdom* that comes with maturity. Taking things in stride, making the right decisions,

expressing yourself with calm authority. Having the confidence to maintain as well as retain your power. "I'm learning to listen to my inner voice and to trust my innate power."

3. The gift of a *balanced mind*. The ability to stay on an even keel regardless of what the addict is up to. "I release others to create their own lives and I create my own through my thoughts, words, and actions."

4. The awareness of *gratitude*. Appreciating the many good things that are in your life. Giving thanks for your health, supportive friends and relatives, your home, your income, and so on. "Each day, I name three positive things that are happening in my life. Today I name (insert x, y, and z)."

5. The *humility* to act in a gentle manner toward others and yourself. Knowing there's no need to harangue the addict in your life. Knowing that it's not necessary to give yourself a hard time, either. "I forgive myself and others."

6. The ability to *let go*. Knowing you can divest yourself of the heavy burden you've taken upon yourself. Realizing there is nothing you could have done, anyway. "I let go and let God."

7. The courage to *trust*. Giving yourself a break and

letting the natural flow of events create a positive change. "I let the goodness of life unfold in its perfect time."

8. The desire to be *healed* and for others to be healed. This is where you can include the addicts. "I honor the healing process working in the lives of all."

9. The *self-control* not to react. You used to be in a bind. The addict would engage you in frustrating, no-win situations and, predictably, you would react. But no more. "I am centered and relaxed and follow my own guidance."

10. The willingness to *think positively* and to give up negative thinking. The realization that negative thinking can only pull you down. "I choose positive, healthy thoughts for my life."

11. The determination to *free yourself* of all victimization. To change the dynamics in your life that place you either at the mercy of the addict or your own troubled brain. "I am free of all victimization."

12. The courage to *love yourself.* To take care of your physical, mental, and spiritual needs. To give yourself the same warmth and affection you would give to a good friend. The strength not to be influenced by what others think of you. "I am worthy of my own love."

Affirmations can include career and financial goals, the need of a new house or car, a vacation in Hawaii. You can even affirm that your addicted children will go into recovery in order to get their lives together. You can create your life the way you would like it to be. Affirmations help you realize your goals. They're a bit like prayers.

And prayers have a way of coming true.

Notes

1. Betty Bethards is the author of *The Dream Book: Symbols For Self-Understanding* and *Seven Steps to Developing Your intuitive Powers* (both from NewCentury Publishers). These books offer many details on how to practice the exercises in this chapter. Betty has also written *Be Your Own Guru*, *There is No Death*, and *Techniques for Health and Wholeness*, again from NewCentury Publishers. For more information on all of Betty's remarkable work, please visit her website at: Innerlight.org.

2. The American Medical Association Encyclopedia of medicine, page 671.

10

Positives of Being the Parent of an Addict

CADEN'S STORY. We sit in Caden's Burbank, California, office on a sunny day and he talks about how his life, values, and perceptions have changed over the course of his son's drug problems.

The son, Mesa, was the typical product of a Hollywood film family (father a producer, mother an actress) who, instead of following the Beverly Hills path paved with privilege, has taken another path. Into drugs. And homicide.

"I thought I knew my son," Caden says, "but I realize now that he was only letting me see what he wanted me to see. The real Mesa ran with a pack of hopped-up Hollywood kids who got their kicks doing terrible things." Caden proceeds to tell me what

some of those terrible things were, the main one being the immolation of a homeless man.

"It was the pain of what happened that shook
my entire world, everything I believed in and
thought I knew," Caden says. On a table near his
desk are a few trappings of his career including the
ultimate prize: the Oscar.

Caden grins. "If it hadn't been for Mesa's problems, I might've had a couple of those by now," he
says. "But you know, when your child is in this kind
of trouble, you find yourself getting in touch with
what really matters. I went from being one of those
guys who lives, eats, and breathes the film business
twenty-four hours a day to someone with, I hope, a
little awareness. I don't feel like the same person I
was, a guy whose values were pretty superficial. But
it took a tragedy to do it."

Mesa, who has just turned fifteen, is in a California correctional facility where he's been for a year
and will be for at least another seven. As is typical
with certain drug addicts who've undergone detoxi-
fication, he has no recall of the past, claims he
doesn't remember any of the events leading up to
his arrest.

"Seeing him in prison is hard," Caden says. "He
looks just like your normal, average teenager. Only
behind bars. And totally vulnerable and scared. It
usually takes me a couple of days to get over each
visit. The first three or four times he begged me to

get him out of there, but he knows now that there's nothing I or anyone else can do. I don't have anything to offer Mesa except honesty—the way I used to be as a parent has changed, all that manipulative ego that goes into being in charge is gone. I'm no longer in charge."

Caden pauses a moment. "I've searched my mind to find out where I may have failed my son. At first I thought it had something to do with his mom and I splitting up. Then I thought it was because I'd spent too much time being a film producer and not enough time being a father. But is this really what led to my son pouring gasoline on someone and then lighting a match? Two of my kids never touched drugs. The third one did. Would he have stayed off them if I'd been more visible? I have no answers.

"What I do know is that I see life in a completely different way now. Before all this happened, very little from the outer world touched me. I drove past it all in my shiny Mercedes. But not any more."

A major positive: the power of choice

If you, as the parent of an addict, think your child has been, or is perhaps currently, victimizing you, answer this for yourself: Who's letting it happen?

Okay, you were confused when your child first became addicted. Then you went through a periods of guilt and grief. But when you came to your senses, why did you let the situation continue? Why didn't you make the necessary changes? Stop the money flow? Call in the police to confiscate your child's drugs? Refuse to bail your child out when your child got into trouble with the law?

If the addict is making your life hell at this moment, why aren't you taking a stand?

The point is, addicts can only do to a parent what the parent allows. An addict can only wrest power away from the parent if the parent agrees to it.

To purge themselves of the victim mentality, parents of addicts must come to a certain, clear realization. They must recognize that they brought (and are possibly still bringing) upon themselves a major chunk of the misery associated with another's chemical addiction. And they're doing this by not honoring their own right to live a normal, peaceful existence. It's easy to castigate the addict with blame. But blame is a means by which a parent avoids taking full responsibility for what has befallen him or her.

To move ahead, we parents of addicts must accept the fact that any harm that came to us was harm we did not block. And any abuse we are currently accepting is abuse we are not turning away.

Once the parent of an addict is cognizant of the situation, there are no excuses to remain stuck. If we choose to remain stuck, victimization must then be seen as self-appointed.

On the other hand, aware parents will come to

appreciate that one of the positives gained through the experience with their addicts is that of choice: having the power to be able to choose what is right for us and what is wrong. And having the power of being able to act upon those choices.

Forgiveness: another positive when used the right way

There is always one person who is deserving of your forgiveness. And that person is you. In fact, self-forgiveness is essential.

Without forgiving themselves, parents of addicts remain in a Never-Never land. Never knowing if they are doing the right thing for themselves. Never knowing if they are doing the right thing for their addicted kids and the rest of their family. Never knowing if the decisions they make in the future will be the right ones.

Forgiveness is a pardon parents can bestow upon themselves for all unwise decisions they have made in the past. It's a wiping clean of the slate. It's also a statement of how far a parent has come. But it takes a while to make that statement.

Before parents of addicted kids embrace the concept of forgiveness, they go through a gamut of emotions: anger, blame, fear, remorse, regret. They judge themselves and others harshly. There is little room for compassion. The drug or alcohol addiction of one's young—and all the ramifications—is all the parent is able to concentrate on. Eventually, there's a shift in the parent's attitude. The parent begins to understand that blame, judgment, and criticism are useless. In the end, how can you blame, judge, or criticize the addict who is sick? Or yourself, the parent, who is powerless to change the situation?

But forgiveness can be used unwisely when it comes to the addict. Each time you give an addict reason to believe he or she is absolved of past and present misconduct, abuse, or violence, that addict will take it that you are condoning these acts, even taking some of the burden upon your own shoulders. This creates—to the addict's way of thinking—the opportunity he or she has been waiting for, which is to continue along the same behavioral route of destruction as before. Offering forgiveness to an active addict is tantamount to inviting a fresh supply of grief into your life.

This does not mean you mustn't forgive the addict. It's simply means that forgiveness of the addict must always be in your heart but—until such a time as the addict successfully completes a recovery program—never on your lips.

Positives that come from pain

Pain is an agent toward enlightenment. The ongoing discomfort, grief, and remorse that coincides with a child's addiction eventually humbles a parent, bringing that parent to his or her knees. It then goes on to create an openness, a willingness to accept. It also brings into being something new and untapped from within the parent: the need to rebuild and revitalize his or her own ravaged life. The emotions, usually so jumbled, seem to reorganize themselves so that the parent feels more in control, more able to deal with the situation at hand.

Out of pain comes lasting positives. Here are some of the most important:

Strength. If a parent can weather the addiction of a child and deal with the upheaval which generally takes place during the crisis and its aftermath, that parent is no longer a novice. There's a healthy determination never to fall victim again to another person's addictive traits. The parent is now able to observe the addictive child from a safely detached place without internalizing the drama or the disappointment or the hopelessness. This is a position of strength parents don't generally achieve before drugs have claimed their kids. This is a result born of anguish.

Confidence. Probably the first trait to vanish when one's child becomes addicted, it has to be coaxed back. But it's never the same old brand of confidence which was based on the ego. This is a no-nonsense form of confidence that doesn't waiver or weaken. The parent possessing it can now make decisions for the right reasons, ones that are rational instead of fearful and guilt-ridden. Confidence is a shield telling the addict that the parent is in a healthy place now and can no longer be manipulated.

Resolve. Addicts will never stop trying to manipulate their parents. They may go underground for awhile, but they continually resurface. Some parents making the split from their addictive kids worry that they'll never see them again. Parents who've gained a healthy resolve know that they will see, or at least hear from their addicted kids every now and then. They know that these kids will periodically try the same old tactics, hoping that this troublesome "resolve" will have died within the parent. Drug addicts and alcoholics don't go away—they just keep coming back to remind us that resolve has to be maintained at all costs.

Courage. When the parent of an addict can walk away from the sickness of his or her child, it's more than just putting one foot in front of the other. It's more like continually forcing aside the crushing pity one feels for the addict so as not to stray from what one knows is right.

Once parents have signaled an end to the dysfunctional way they've previously dealt with an addict, and have pulled—with every ounce of pluck, spunk, mettle, and grit—against the emotional parent/child chains that bind, they can think of themselves as truly intrepid beings, worthy of the highest acclaim.

Positives that come with letting go

The option of letting go is something parents discover when recognizing that they are powerless to change anything or anyone but themselves. What's nice about letting go is that we can turn over all problems and people and see everything as happening for the best.

Many parents become spiritual only through adversity. But it doesn't matter how they get to this crossroads, as long as they get there.

One of the most positive results of having an addicted child is the comfort and peace you will feel once you've accepted the fact that you are powerless. You even begin to wonder where you ever got the idea that you had so much influence in the first place.

Ultimately, we can thank our children for being such wonderful teachers. For, without them, we might still be slaves to our egos. We might still be pandering to the demanding voices within ourselves, the voices we've obeyed for so many years.

Our addicted children brought out the best in us. Their involvement in a ghastly and dangerous obsession has led us to freedom—if we wish to accept it.

Positives that come from learning to live again

A major change occurs when the parent of an addict switches off the victim role and takes on an entirely new identity, that of the strong, highly-resolved individual who knows there's life after drugged kids.

For one thing, the parent feels a surge of freedom that is exhilarating. It's like emerging into bright sunshine after many years in a dark cell. For another, the parent will now be able to pick up the pieces of his or her broken life, start new projects, meet new people, *do all those things that have been delayed.*

Here are some of the bonuses awaiting the newly liberated parent.

Happiness. A simple word, but how many parents of addicts can honestly apply it to themselves? When that old "but I'm his parent" philosophy finally bites the dust, the first (often unrecognizable) feelings of happiness can take place. This is not a happiness brought about by success in a job or a winning lottery ticket or any other outside force. It comes from knowing that you've finally freed yourself and are allowing your addicted offspring to do the same. Congratulations.

Peace of mind. Remember that? Well, it comes back again in a whole new way. Simply by letting go of the job you had so rigidly held onto, your mind can be free to think of things other than addicted children, violence, manipulation, and abuse. This can happen when you've turned your mind from the past. As with happiness, you may not recognize the feeling associated with peace right away. But it'll catch on, and when it does, you won't want to be without it ever again.

Trust. Neither happiness nor peace of mind are possible without trust. Just the idea that we don't have to worry about our addicted children any more is a form of bliss. So who's taking care of them if we're not? Call it a higher power, the same source that's taking care of *all* of us.

Can there be any positives for an addicted child?

It's hard to believe that there could be. But there's a lot to be learned from a drug addict or alcoholic. The experience of being a drug addict or alcoholic can definitely serve humankind. As it turns out, some of the only people qualified to call themselves authorities on the subject of substance abuse are former substance abusers themselves. Only the former addict can tell you how the mind of a drug addict works. That's because he or she has been there. And we haven't. Nor have many of the so-called expert psychologists and counselors. As in any trade, it's best to have some degree of education. Former addicts got their education from the substances they abused. As the escalation of drug-use hits an all time high worldwide, there will be an increasing need for these former addicts who've actually been "in the field" and can counsel the steady flow of younger addicts.

Counselors who have been addicts are usually better able to detect the manipulations or scams devised so cleverly by practicing addicts. As these counselors will testify, they probably know every move an addict is making or is planning to make. Didn't they do the same?

So perhaps there is a positive to your child being an addict. Perhaps your child is being trained to counsel others. Maybe the streets and the alleys are his or her classroom. On staff at practically every rehab in every city across this country, there will be at least several people who've gained an education living the life of a junkie or a drunk. These are invaluable personnel, people who've walked into the darkness and have walked out again.

Could be this is where your addicted child is headed?

How about you? Can you help others?

There are many child-psychology experts out there making valuable contributions to our culture. But unless they've taken the same roller-coaster ride that the parent of an addict has taken, they can't speak from experience on this topic.

Experience doesn't always count for everything. But once the parent of an addict has passed a certain stage, the "letting-go stage," he or she can relate to other parents in trouble and offer help. After all, who knows better the pain and sorrow of seeing a child in such distress than the parent?

It's not that I don't have the greatest respect for professionals or feel that there isn't a huge need for them: It's just that there's a big difference in "living it" and "learning it." Not long ago, I attended a three-hour seminar given by a noted child psychologist. His subject was how to deal with teenagers so that they wouldn't fall into the clutches of drugs and alcohol. I was curious about his methods—which consist mainly of "talking" to young addicts and "talking' to them some more.

Then he mentioned that his own children were two and three years old. Listening to him, I wondered just how much his methods in dealing with young people would change over the years, especially after his children reached puberty.

It will be interesting to hear what he has to say in a decade or two.

EPILOGUE

Just When You Thought You'd Wised-up, the Phone Rings

ALL OUR STORIES. When you're the parent of a drug addict or alcoholic, you learn a lot. You learn to be on your guard so that you cannot be manipulated in any shape, way, or form by the addict. You learn to treat yourself like a human being after all these years of treating yourself as a non-being. You become articulate, telling the addict exactly what you are prepared to do for him or her (lend moral support if he or she will get into recovery) and what you are not prepared to do (lend money, your car, your home, your TV, the kitchen clock, the list is endless). You even congratulate yourself when the addict, knowing you are extremely well versed as to his or her ways, doesn't try to get you into a corner quite as often, if at all.

Somewhere in your mind is the possibility that

perhaps the addict will never bug you again, that perhaps those days are over at long last, that perhaps the addict has finally got a job, got a life.

And then the phone rings. Guess who's on the line asking how you are, how the rest of the family is, asking if the recent storm caused any damage to the house, asking if your sprained back from ten years before has been acting up, and while he or she is at it, asking for a loan of five thousand dollars?

There is no doubt in my mind that even if you were to tell the addict that the house burned down and that you and the rest of your family were now destitute, living off charity, and wondering where your next meal was coming from, the addict's only comment would be: "Yeah, but what about the five thousand dollars?"

I've been caught off guard more than a few times, as has just about every addict's parent that I know of. Drug abuse and alcoholism seem to rob addicts of any consideration for anyone, starting with themselves. While you're enjoying the hiatus from their demands, addicts aren't, as much as you'd like to think, out there becoming altruistic. They're out there waiting for the right moment to spring yet one more request upon you. As far as they're concerned —who knows, maybe during that long period they haven't called you—you've revised your stand on not giving them your hard earned cash. It's certainly worth a try, isn't it?

Thinking of myself as implacable when it came to the requests made of me by the addicts in my life, I was shocked to find myself caught in the same old position. One day recently the phone woke me up a little before dawn. Not having heard from this particular addicted child for quite some time, my main reaction was surprise. Didn't the fact that he was calling me at this strange hour give me a clue that nothing had really changed? And didn't I have a speech ready to recite in regard to the hurt I felt at never having received a Christmas card or a birthday card or a Father's Day card? Or even a thank-you card for the Christmas and birthday cards I'd sent, accompanied by generous, hockable gifts?

Luckily, I was ready for the inevitable question that I *knew* would be coming right after all the How-are-yous. And when it came I was able to say no and get off the phone.

But close friends whom I'll call Jane and Neal, the parents of a drug-addicted son, weren't let off the hook (no pun intended) as easily. When their son called after months of no communication asking for a loan, they found themselves actually saying yes! As veterans of some grotesque scenes with this particular son, they'd been fully prepared to reject any and all further pleas of financial help. And here they were, all reason seeming to have abandoned them, agreeing to lend their son a sizeable chunk of money. This was to be, assured the son, just a loan—

one that would be returned to them in just two weeks. With interest.

There had been quite a few other promises made in the past by the addict to repay the sizeable chunks. With interest. Needless to say, the parents had never seen one cent returned.

Over the course of the next few hours Jane and Neal questioned themselves about what had happened. They realized that, for some reason, they'd regressed into the parents they used to be. Had they not learned anything after all this time in dealing with an addict? Was their newly found strength just a facade? The money they'd supplied in the past had enabled their son to drug himself senseless, and he'd only be doing it again with funds Jane and Neal provided via Western Union.

Still wanting to help: It's a parent thing

All loving parents want nothing more than to be able to help their children. Sometimes we—as parents of drug addicts and alcoholics—forget that, when it comes to money, this is impossible. Jane and Neal, recovering from their oversight, and feeling bad that they'd made the promise, realized they'd have to renege. When their son telephoned inquiring as to why the money hadn't been sent, Jane and Neal screwed up their courage and told him simply that they'd changed their minds.

Suddenly, the son who'd been fairly pleasant up

until that point wasn't so pleasant any more. A blast
of venom came over the line revealing the son's
drug-state. When the venom had no effect, the son
went into a series of manipulative moves which had
no effect, either. Jane and Neal couldn't be swayed,
although their legs went weak and it felt as if their
hearts were being ripped out of their chests.

This was their own beloved son calling in the
dead of winter from some town in Michigan saying
he didn't even have a coat to wear or a roof over his
head. But Jane and Neal stayed firm and said no.

Their son, knowing he'd got nowhere, then told
his parents he was going to commit suicide. Jane
and Neal had no reply for that—wasn't he committing suicide every day of his life by being on drugs?
And then came his last attempt to coerce. He told
Jane and Neal that they would never again hear
from him, that they didn't have a son. Which is
when Neal let him have it.

"What son?" Neal retorted in anger. "When
have you been a son? When do we ever hear from
you, except when you want money? As far as we're
concerned, you're not our son, you're just some drug
or other calling me long distance collect."

By the time Neal got off the phone, he was shaking. But he and Jane had won. They had managed to
defeat that harmful, codependent side of themselves
which had kept them locked in a to-the-death embrace not with their son, but with the drugs that

controlled him and had made him into the pitiful creature he was.

The son's parting words had stung Jane and Neal the most: that they were finks for having said they would send the money and had then backed out, just as they'd backed out on every single agreement they'd ever made, just as they'd backed out on being a mother and father to him from the time he was born. As friends of Jane and Neal and knowing the love and care they gave this son as he was growing up, I knew this wasn't true. But did Jane and Neal?

"The one thing we really feel bad about," Neal confided in me later, "was that we told him yes and then told him no."

"You changed your mind, that's all," I tell him. "And that has to be okay."

Addicts can change their minds, but parents of addicts can't?

How many times has your addicted child promised to do something for you and has then failed to live up to it? Promises such as taking out the trash, washing the car, repaying the $50 loan for the CDs, repaying the $1500 for the stereo, getting the wall plastered up where he bashed his fist into it while under the influence of drugs or alcohol? Too many times to count?

How many times have you promised to do something for the addict and gone through hell and high water to keep that promise? How about the time you took out a loan so you could raise bail when the addict ran afoul of the law? Too many other times to count?

Parents of addicts tend to think they have to live up to every word they say, even when the addicts show repeatedly that they have no intention whatsoever of honoring their own commitments.

You might say that these addicts simply changed their minds. Several thousand times. But when their parents do it once or twice, they beat themselves senseless with guilt. Worse, they let the addicts do it for them.

This is the crux of the dilemma in the parent/ addict relationship, and it has nothing at all to do with the addict. It has to do with the inability of parents to recognize their own misplaced familial loyalty. Many parents of addicts feel they must fulfill all rescue missions, a disease in itself. It is from this rigidity that parents of addicts decrease their chances of feeling good about themselves And incidentally, the chances of the addict ever seeking recovery.

In the end, it's the fear of letting the addict down and the shame of being accused by the addict of being a fink that keeps parents and addicts stuck in the worst kind of human drama.

Variations on a tired, old theme

Here's another example of addict manipulation that

plagues parents. The phone rings. It's the addict. He says he has a job. You're thrilled. But you're also apprehensive. Because you know he hasn't simply called to tell you good news. That kind of thing just doesn't happen. Then comes the zinger you knew would be coming. The request. He says everybody at this company wears business suits and ties, none of which he has. He says if you can't wire him $1800 right away, he won't be able to take the job. The implications are clear.

Suddenly, you've become the deciding factor as to whether or not the addict will be able to take the job. Have a future. Have a life.

You've got that old, familiar sick feeling in the pit of your stomach. This is not the child you gladly would have financed in any way possible to get him started in life. This is the child who has been strung out on drugs for years and has shown absolutely no interest in such things as having a conventional job. He has also, if you remember correctly, come to you quite a few times with variations on this same tired, old story. One variation called for a car so he could get to work. (Why is it that addicts are always being offered jobs in the middle of nowhere that can't be reached by public transportation?) Another variation called for the money to purchase a round-trip airline ticket to interview for a job three thousand miles away. Being presented with what amounts to a no-choice request, the question is: Are you going to contribute in what you know is probably another scam, or are you going to say sorry and hang up?

To step out of the role of banker/victim/rescuer, you have to quit the job of banker/victim/rescuer. You have to change the coda. You have to forget all the stipulations there are to being a parent. You have to harden your heart and tell yourself parenthood no longer applies to you—not while your child is addicted. Not an easy thing to do.

P.S. You know in your heart there is no job starting on Monday. But even if there is, it's hardly your responsibility if the addict goes well dressed, badly dressed, or undressed.

Facing the unfaceable: The situation may never change

In summary, you had a child and that child became an addict. Your love for the child didn't vanish. But you've had to wean yourself away from the person your child has become through his or her drugs and/or alcohol abuse. Your journey with the addicted child has led you through various stages of pain, grief, and despair and into new phases of strength, acceptance, and healing. There's a good chance that you might not be as healthy-minded as you are today had it not been for the tribulations with the addict. But you'll never know. The one thing you do know is that you wouldn't volunteer to go through it again, even with all the awareness you've gained. You would never have sacrificed your child just so that you could become a better, stronger person.

But this is the way it has turned out. You're doing okay with it, almost twenty-four hours a day. It's just the odd few minutes that are hard to get through, like the ones in the middle of the night when you awaken to find that the grief hasn't really gone away—it's just under smart, new management. Or when you're walking along a street or in a mall and you see someone who reminds you of your addicted child, but isn't a substance abuser, and you feel that void in your heart. You ache for what might have been with your child, the happy life, the fulfilled career. And you ache for the events that never took place—the high school graduation, the engagement party, the wedding, the grandkids. These are the celebrations of life that you'll probably never get to enjoy.

Although you never know.

DON'T LET YOUR KIDS KILL YOU

*A Guide for Parents
of Drug and Alcohol
Addicted Children*

PART 2

1

Go Ahead Back in... If You Dare

Luke's story. I'm sitting with Luke, who is sixty-two years old, the widowed father of three children, all of whom have been estranged from him for quite some time. His late wife, Louise, was an unrecovered alcoholic and codependent. Through the bad press from Louise, he has been painted as an uncaring father who was also someone who wouldn't ever part with a cent to help his kids.

These charges, Luke says, are completely false. He has been bailing out his kids for ages, but after each rescue, everyone seems to have total memory loss, and he is right back where he started.

Recently, Luke has had contact with one of these children, Linda, aged twenty-five (the other two live far away and are never in touch). Linda has had a long history of drug abuse but, with Luke's help, successfully completed a drug rehab program. This assistance went unacknowledged by Linda as did all the other things Luke did for her. It seemed her only interest in staying in contact was to get money out of him. And whenever he would call a halt, she would drop out of his life.

"Maybe I was crazy this time," Luke says, "or just hopeful. But I wanted to see if anything had changed with my daughter over the past couple of years. It had changed as far as her not being on drugs any longer, but hadn't as far as money went. By the third meeting with Linda, I was in the bag for $10,000".

I asked Luke the pertinent question to which I got an affirmative answer. "Were you tying to buy her back?"

When parents get to a certain stage of recovery, there's a very tricky period when a relapse can happen at any moment.

One of the signs of this happening is when the subject at a reunion revolves around money and nothing else. You want to talk about love and affection for each other, and the family and healing and all things positive, and, meanwhile, there's your child droning on and on about money and the need for money and the promise that, if you will only supply the money, it will be paid back (payday after next is the usual time frame). Of course a debt of $10,000 would have to be paid back over many future paydays.

The strange thing about the Luke/Linda dialogue is that Luke, due to early retirement, makes quite a bit less than Linda who, when working, makes a good living as a waitress. Probably twice or three times as much as Luke does.

"It should be me asking her for a loan instead of me handing over my life savings on the bet that this will bring us closer."

I asked Luke why he agreed and his reply is classic in this kind of situation: "Because she is off drugs and does work and has several kids and one of them needs medical care and there's no insurance. I feel she is trying her best and that's something different from the way she was before."

"Haven't you had that feeling a number of times before when forking over money?" I ask.

"Many times, and I've lost track of the money I've doled out." Luke reports wearily. "Those old debts are never discussed."

"Any reason they're not?" I ask, but I already know the answer.

"I stay away from anything having to do with the past," Luke says, obviously afraid of losing Linda for a bunch more years. "I'm sixty-two. Over the past ten or twelve years, I would say I've only had Linda in my life for a month here and few months there. And then she would be away and I never knew if she was dead or alive. A couple of times she was almost dead from overdoses. I would always hate it when the phone rang late at night. There had been so many times when Linda was in the hospital or in jail. Then I developed a heart condition and had to have triple by-pass. My stress was over the top."

I think it but don't have to say it, that Linda's actions certainly didn't help his health.

"The final clincher," Luke continues "was when my wife died and became the martyr and I became the forever bad guy."

There is always, I have found, a "forever bad guy" in these unfortunate family scenarios. This is usually the non-enabler, the person who simply won't go along with the sick routine. At other times, it is just a family member like Luke who has done some codependent deeds on occasion and who happens to have "target" written all over him or herself. It seems those people abusing substances need someone upon whom to heap blame and abuse.

"Has Linda been in touch since the $10,000 loan?" I ask.

The look on Luke's face says it all. "The last I've seen or heard of her was two months ago and I haven't heard a peep since. I call but never get her in. My messages are not answered. I had to go into the hospital with a new ailment—enlarged prostate and the inability to urinate, and I left her a message asking if she would visit me, and heard nothing. Tried her line again last week and her phone has been disconnected."

Obviously the "payday after next" story didn't

pan out either.

"I don't know..." Luke says. "I think I was doing better before I tried to get back in touch with my daughter. At least I was accustomed somewhat to not having contact and," he adds, "I was $10,000 richer."

Always remember: They will ALWAYS be smarter than you

They have lived on the street and they know all the angles. They have done mostly anything to get drugs which makes for a most impressive counter-lifestyle resume.

How can you possibly compete with them in terms of experience? Have you ever stolen money from your parents and friends, hocked their valu-ables, sold you body, begged people for their spare change, shoplifted, or gone in for far more serious criminal activities?

From what I've seen, many of these people have expert criminal mentalities, and once you re-connect, it's like being manacled and held hostage. Freeing yourself again is an arduous process in which they dispense guilt as if it is going out of style. The victim usually feels remorse, regret and sorrow along with the guilt. There is a complete halt to you doing anything advantageous for yourself during this time. After all, why should you have a good life and funds in the bank and a peaceful existence if they are, as they say, suffering, even starving to death, ill, and practically homeless?

What kind of monster are you, anyway, that would put a crust of bread in your mouth while they are allegedly eating out of garbage cans?

Suicide, they will often tell their victims, is the way they are headed—and their victims recoil in horror at the thought.

They know how to persuade, charm, wheedle, and squeeze money from you, from relatives, from friends, from senior citizens, from strangers.

They've dealt with hardened drug dealers, lived in squalid conditions without caring, smuggled drugs, have been on the run from the law, been arrested and jailed, been in complete blackouts, and yes, have eaten out of garbage cans.

Their scams have been ingenious—you have no idea. Had they turned their minds to positive endeavors, who knows, one of them might have discovered the cure for cancer.

And you think you're smarter than they are?

For these people, that decent, moral wiring of the brain is absent. Even when drugs and alcohol are not in the picture any longer there is still the "I can get anything I want from you" mindset at work. Being clean and sober doesn't mean the scheming and the scams are retired to some dusty trunk of memories. In most cases all they have to do is put on an innocent face, mouth some positive senti- ments that they know you want to hear, and there you go, not being able to wait to write a check.

When they are determined in getting what they want, they are armed with all sorts of ploys and they are a great threat to you peace of mind. For them, you are nothing but an innocent babe, no matter how hard you try to outguess or outmaneuver them. And when you don't comply, remember this: You are nothing but a piece of disposable matter.

If this sounds harsh, it's for your own good. You have to see these scheming children as you would see a mugger. And never let down your guard. Or else you can make up your mind to live your life as a Brinks money bag with legs.

When kids do drugs they often stay kids.

Aside from children who are out to take from you everything you have, there is yet another heartbreaking reality. This has to do with kids who fail to mature due to the drugs they took at an young age. According to medical experts, taking drugs early on can mean that these individuals may retain an immature nature sometimes lasting for the rest of their lives.

Even if they come off drug dependency and are admitted back into society as clean and sober they may not be able to pick up the pieces and continue a normal growth pattern. They may be squeaky clean physically, but as for their mental and emotional health, many former drug users are permanently disabled. If you expect them to take responsibility for themselves, don't hold your breath. If you expect them to stop blaming you and others, don't hold your breath. Chances are they will react to you as a spoiled and sullen adolescent might.

And outside the home and your sphere of influence, they may have trouble adjusting to a job routine or a meaningful relationship. The whole chronology of graduating high school, going to college, getting married and having children of their own may be grievously upset. Simply put, they tend not to act with the maturity of same-age contemporaries.

Meanwhile, you may still be in a state of frustration and despair because you believed that once your child was off substances, he or she would just start acting like a normal, rational, mature, reasonable, hard-working, conscientious human being.

If that favorable scenario is not exactly the case, or if it's not even close to being the case, you need to check your emotions and come to terms with the situation as it is, not as you would like it to be.

Another addiction of the young that afflicts parents

Gambling. Kids don't have to shoot up for this—it's already in the blood. And parents of gamblers are like parents of drug and alcohol abusers. Distressed. The age-old practice of gambling, romanticized in this country by the lure of the river boats of old, and the Las Vegases of today, has now become a major addiction that can, and often does, accompany drug and alcohol misuse. I get call after call from parents whose kids not only abuse substances, but go out and gamble everything away while under the influence.

With an all-time interest in gambling these days, the experience of risking everything has become something of a thrill for countless young people. They give it the time and attention others might give a career.

As of this writing, gambling has not yet been exposed as the insidious habit-forming villain it really is. It's not as visible as, say, the obesity epidemic sweeping America–something you can't miss. But it is happening and many young people are frittering away their potentials. All the more reason for parents to steer clear as much as possible and to pile on the positive stuff they are doing for themselves.

A word about the recovered child

Obviously, we shouldn't lump children who've recovered in with those who haven't. If the child has proved to be responsible, it's another story. Most parents want to help their kids if possible, and a child who has cleaned up his or her act is as trustworthy as a kid that hasn't had to.

Kids formerly thought lost to drugs can not only recover, but they often go on to do impressive things in all walks of life.

For example, many of the drug counselors in treatment centers and rehabs were once addicted to, or dependent upon, substances themselves. Through their own experiences in having done drugs, having lived on the streets, and having employed truly questionable behavior, they possess an uncanny X-ray vision one can only acquire from having been in exactly the same place as their clients. Addicts cannot pull the wool over the eyes of these counselors because these counselors been in exactly the same situations themselves, giving them the ability to read, with amazing accuracy, the mind of a druggie.

A ray of hope

Interestingly, quite a few of these counselors were once thought of as hopeless addicts when, in fact, they were basically, and very badly, dependent on drugs–rather than truly addicted. They were dependent, that is, to the very point of addiction. But having been able to get off drugs showed that, despite all the earmarks of being addicts, and with all the negative traits of addicts, they were able to escape a fate that probably would have kept them prisoners of drugs for the rest of their lives.

People are often mistaken for addicts when in truth it's because they exhibit all the signs of addicts. From what I've seen, if they can eventually, with a lot of work, walk away from drugs, they have a chance of a good life.

This could be the case with your child.

2

Health Matters

A portable comfort station

My story again. I may have written *Don't Let Your Kids Kill You*, but on the various occasions when I've fallen off the recovery cart, my sister in New York would chirp "don't let your kids kill you" in a rather irritating singsong voice.

At other times, when I've been in a woeful mood, I've been told by friends "Charles, read your book". I do re-read it regularly because I know my kids were/are my drug of choice.

Don't Let your Kids Kill you is a portable comfort station. Many people regard it as a best friend.

Safeguarding your heart

The heart of a loving parent is different from other

hearts. It's fragile, hopeful, watchful, forgiving and all too often, defenseless. The relationships parents have with their kids are not like the ones they have with others--be it a wife, husband, mother, father, sibling, lover or friend. The human heart can ache over a faithless lover, a cheating mate, or by the death of a spouse or sweetheart, but even then, the breakage is not like the breakage felt by a parent whose child is on drugs.

For loving parents, their kids, no matter what age, are vulnerable and potentially always in harm's way. We feel that with our hearts. I know I am continually white-lighting my kids—which I consider a form of prayer. The parent role is that of the protector, the cushion a child can fall back on, the person who, for that child, would give his or her very life.

Our children come from our bodies and stay in our bodies. They stay in our minds and hearts. No matter how parents try to rationalize that they are separate from their kids, it is my opinion that they are fooling themselves. There is no separation. Is there separation between you and the arm that hangs at you side, the nose on your face? The bond with a child is a heart bond. It is there forever.

This is the connection that leads to our suffering. The Buddhists have a saying that applies to all relationships as "The ripening of poisonous fruit". When our children are born and when they are growing up, there is such joy and pleasure and closeness, but as time goes on, and children make their way in the world, the pressure upon a loving parent's heart increases. The worry and concerns over the knocks and falls a child takes in life becomes major jolts to the heart. Perhaps not always major in a conscious way, but major, nevertheless.

And when the child does things that are self-destructive, that's when the poison seeps in. No longer is the former closeness and love available to you. All of this takes a toll on the heart—and there isn't a parent alive (or dead) that hasn't experienced this unwanted and unpleasant sensation, even with relatively positive children.

So it is important to protect the heart. A broken heart can rob us of our vitality and interest in living. It can destroy our health. It can eventually kill us. Those palpitations aren't there for nothing. That ache in the heart at four in the morning is a strong signal that something has to change if we don't want to die. The heart of a loving parent revolves around the knowledge that that child is safe and happy. If that isn't forthcoming and the child is in serious trouble due to drugs or some other reason, a gray cloud of despair descends upon the parent. What's the best way to protect one's heart? I have devised a way for myself that I would like to share with you.

The Black Magic Marker Line

The most telling stress indicators in the human

body are in the solar plexus where fear and worry reside, and in the heart, a gauge that lets us know how much stress we're under because it aches when it is breaking. Sometimes the palpitations are so severe, one fears for his or her life.

Not wanting to die, I realized at a certain point in my life that it is up to me to protect my heart. There are things I do to relieve stress—such as daily meditation and exercise and getting involved in work and people and in various activities. It's useless to say I don't feel physical manifestations when my kids are having problems, because I do feel them, and these manifestations can be all the more stronger the more serious the problem.

To counter these emotional eruptions and to protect my health, I have created something that works for me. All it takes is some paper and a black magic marker.

Each day, upon awakening, I take a piece of the paper and I draw a thick black line down the center of it. The left section of the page represents my own sacred space. The right section of the page represents my children's sacred space. And never, as the saying goes, the twain shall meet. Except in harmony.

With this device, the problems of my children remain the problems of my children. Instead of becoming lost in their drama, I stay centered. Instead of forgetting about my own life and instead of allowing the palpitations and chest pains and headaches to take over, I have a healthy barrier which lets me concentrate on such things as the other members of my family, job, career, friends, interests, and fun– remember fun? And, as I've stated before in this book, when my life is in order, I become a strong role model for the addicted child.

Symbolically, the black magic marker line separates your stuff from the stuff of others so that you can have some sort of life. On your side of the page, you can list all your projects, aspirations, self-nurturing habits and all else that is positive in your life. You needn't bother about the right side of the page. Frankly, you have no business even being on that side of the page, and others have no business being on your side the page. Physical, emotional, and financial trespassing is not allowed.

There's a very good reason why the word "magic" is in the product name of this very useful marker.

It really works magic.

Your job on earth.

It's very simple. To be happy, healthy, and to love and know yourself. No matter what. That way, you can also help others.

3

Wanna Make a Difference in the World?

Up until now, the format of this book has been to start each chapter with a case study involving parents of a child abusing drugs or alcohol. But I'm starting this chapter somewhat differently. This case study focuses on our homes, towns, cities, and our country because they are all in danger of becoming drug-ridden disaster areas.

Some states are already on the way to becoming over-run by the drug pandemic. Methamphetamines are now common, even dangerously ho-hum and old hat in many communities. Alarmingly, it's not even as if this drug is being imported; it's being made right at home, while, of course, the usual array of drugs are brought in.

What has followed has been a descent into crime

that's not always publicized with the appropriate tone of importance or urgency. There are areas that depend on a degree of silence as real estate prices might fall were the seriousness of drugs and crime to be out in the open. And in a state, such as Hawai`i, where a weather forecast of rain might be ruinous to the economy, can you imagine what could happen if word got out about the drugs and crime? Scratch any state or, for that matter, any country, and the problem persists, even in remote towns, villages and outposts.

Conversely, just as some information is kept quiet, other information is, unfortunately, given out freely. In California (and presumably elsewhere in this country) a recent cinema commercial actually gave the audience instructions on how to make methamphetamines and where to get the ingredients. The spot then finished with the lame tagline: Don't Do Drugs. How much of that information was later acted upon by the younger audience members is a guess, but the chances are that there were some interested parties.

On another occasion, I was being interviewed on a San Francisco Bay Area call-in radio station. Some callers were surprisingly irate with my stand against drugs. After the broadcast, I was roundly castigated by the show's hosts whom, as I eventually found out, were not only users of recreational drugs, but who also held regular "pot parties" to which their children were invited.

These are just three instances of a tragic situation and there are countless others that proliferate day in and out without resolve.

But there is one weapon that would seriously challenge the spread and the usage of drugs in our communities, and that weapon is right here and right now. Read on.

Introducing a potentially revolutionary weapon against drugs: YOU!

Throughout this book, I have shown how parents are not responsible for the drug situation. Now I'd like to reverse that just a little bit. Because, ironically, and in one very real sense, parents do play a part in the drug plague. And they do this, quite innocently, through the act of anonymity.

Each day there are thousands of secret meetings all over the country. They're called Al Anon, Nar Anon, Tough Love, Parents Anonymous, Parents Supporting Parents, etc. These are miraculously healing and totally necessary meetings, but no one outside of the four walls of those meeting places knows or will ever know the wealth of information that is generated by the people sharing.

Parents attend these anonymous meetings to testify as to the horrors brought about by substance-abusing children. They also listen to other parents testifying, and they then go home, often with the tools of recovery, and the comforting thought that they are not alone in their desperation and pain.

But imagine what might happen if the walls of all those meeting places suddenly dissolved and that thousands, maybe even millions, of people agreed to expose their pain and grief as well as their wisdom and knowledge to the outside world?

And what if all of those people took a stand, much as the Mothers (and I'm sure, fathers) Against Drunk Drivers did, and in the immortal words of Peter Finch in the movie "Network" (1976) cried out: "I'm mad as hell and I'm not going to take this anymore"!

When I wrote "Don't let Your Kids Kill You" I endured a huge amount of criticism for not keeping my mouth shut. My intention was, and is, to teach parents how to live a life of meaning despite the grueling distractions of a beloved child on drugs. Some people (thankfully few) reacted to me as if I was a pariah for having exposed the utter and complete destruction of my family due to drugs and alcohol. Some of my critics set about creating further havoc for me personally—including one with a hit and run approach that riled up even further grievous problems for my family.

My sin was that I had broken the seal of secrecy, the unwritten law which states that one must protect others' wrongdoing through rigid silence. But whom, I wondered, was I supposed to be protecting? Those abusing drugs? Their families? Their dealers? All of the above?

When family members remain silent they are aiding, in the long run, drug traffikers, along with our trusted public servants who take bribes, and the drug cartels themselves.

Most families with kids on drugs are loathe to express their views outside of the 12-Step arena or with very trusted friends and family. But by not revealing the horror stories they are living to the outer world, the bottom line is that they're not only hiding from view the ugly truth of how their lives have disintegrated, but worse, they're actually protecting the very people fueling this disaster.

If there is one reassuring factor that keeps those who supply the drugs happy, it's the silence in which they work. Do they want a mess of parents and legislators and lawmen on their backs exposing their unconscionable work? Doubtful. As long as they can get to our children, make the exchange, pocket the money, and disappear (until next time), they've had a successful transaction.

It's interesting to note how parents will go to great lengths to keep sexual predators out of a neighborhood, how they will go on protest marches, speak on TV, and do anything to get heard. But there is hardly any action taken in giving a true picture of what goes on in the home when a child is on drugs, nor how it affects the family.

If my lone voice did so much good writing this book, think what a hundred thousand voices could do. Here are some ideas:

More mouth, more muscle

Being naked in front of a lot of people isn't comfortable. Exposing your family secret isn't, either. Know this: There's a chance you'll be criticized, but once you open up publicly, you'll find it easier and easier to talk to others about the situation. Chances are that other parents in a similar fix will look you up and pretty soon you may have a neighborhood network consciously keeping the tentacles of drug culture away from your front yards.

It's amazing how an idea can snowball. If enough people are willing to expand their boundaries, many others will feel safe enough to join them. But it all starts with you. And your mouth.

Don't want to talk? Write. Starting with your congressman. Write a letter stating the conditions under which you are living and what you have in mind regarding drug control and reform. Be clear and concise. A polite form letter reply from that particular office (and it usually is the office and rarely the individual) will no doubt come your way. It will inform you that your concerns have been noted, and you will be thanked for writing. This kind of letter obviously isn't worth the paper it's written on.

Repeated letters and emails and even telephone calls might rouse, if nothing else, some frustration on their parts. Aside from writing your congressman, write the newspapers, both local and national. Letters to the Editors are also popular platforms for discussion.

Margaret Mead, the noted anthropologist once stated: "Never doubt that a small group of thoughtful, committed citizens can change the world. Indeed, that's the only thing that ever has."

What war on drugs?

The term "war on drugs" is catchy, but empty. Yes, there are drug raids and there are the seizures of the drugs being brought into the country, and people are busted by the score, and our jails are full of offenders, but in general, there is no plan that really solves the this extraordinarily complex social problem.

Such a plan would involve the public. Instead of the "shock-value" TV and print campaigns that garner awards for the ad agencies that create them (and that are rarely effective), we need valuable information and updates and HELP hotlines and government agencies that partner parents in order to combat the ruinous effects of drugs in our homes and communities. In others words, we need concrete and substantial evidence that something is being done.

Parting words

In refashioning the first step in a 12-Step program, the following words come to mind: I've become powerless over the overwhelming love I feel for my children and my life has become unmanageable.

You have it within you to defeat those forces

that make your life unmanageable. Getting a grip is all it takes, and the knowledge that you were not put here on earth to suffer.

Everyone has a path. Many years ago, I became conscious of the fact that I had to get off my children's case so that they could do what they had to do—and so that I could do what I had to do.

Whether any of my most precious family would survive was questionable, but I did what I felt I was being directed to do. I got out of the way so my children could grow. And I am very, very happy to say that those drug-dependent children have come a long way. They have been off drugs for some years now and they lead productive, happy lives.

Each day that I work on my own problem of codependence is a day in which I become stronger. I draw the magic marker line and accept the challenges that I personally face, rather than the challenges my children face, although I am there for them when their needs are within healthy limits.

Mainly, I am grateful. Life, even in its harshest form, has something to teach. And the gifts are tremendous.

Thank you for reading what I've had to say.

INDEX

Lists of Valuable Information